Excellence in Biling
A Guide for School Principals

The **Cambridge Teacher** series

Peeter Mehisto

CAMBRIDGE
UNIVERSITY PRESS

WORKING WITH

UNIVERSITY *of* CAMBRIDGE
International Examinations

CAMBRIDGE UNIVERSITY PRESS
Cambridge, New York, Melbourne, Madrid, Cape Town,
Singapore, São Paulo, Delhi, Mexico City

Cambridge University Press
The Edinburgh Building, Cambridge CB2 8RU, UK

www.cambridge.org
Information on this title: www.cambridge.org/9781107681477

First published 2012
3rd printing 2012

Printed in the United Kingdom by Printondemand-worldwide, Peterborough

A catalogue record for this publication is available from the British Library

ISBN 978-1-107-68147-7 Paperback

Contents

About the author

Peeter Mehisto, PhD, has worked internationally with a wide variety of stakeholders to develop and manage bilingual programmes. Generating strategic plans and work-plans, building teacher-training programmes, managing public relations and creating learning materials have been integral to these initiatives. Through the University of London, Peeter Mehisto has researched factors contributing to successful bilingual programme development, as well as potential barriers to their implementation. Peeter has researched the benefits of bilingualism. He has taught at primary, secondary and university levels and is the winner of several awards in education. Currently, his primary focuses are the training of teachers and administrators, and consulting on bilingual programme development. His publications, including an award-winning book, have been addressed to educators and to the research community.

Acknowledgements

This work builds on that of many researchers and practitioners in the fields of bilingual education, education and management. The following people deserve thanks for their much-appreciated feedback, input and/or suggestions: Hugo Baetens Beardsmore, Jim Cummins, Jane Deluzio, Al Monshateh Dira, Fred Genesee, Conrad Hughes, Sue Hughes, Jim Johnston, Sandra Lucietto, David Marsh, Syeda Madiha Murshed, Valeri Novikov, Andre Piketh, Silvia Rettaroli and Ejigayehu Zewdie. A thank you is also extended to teachers and students for their anonymous inputs, to designer Tõnis Kärema and to editor Helen Imam. In addition, colleagues at University of Cambridge International Examinations and at Cambridge University Press deserve special thanks for their valuable suggestions.

Photos on page 4 © iStockphoto.com/Sean Locke, Robert Churchill, jabejon.

Acknowledging the expertise of practitioners, University of Cambridge International Examinations invites principals of bilingual schools to share their experience of implementing bilingual education as well as their views on this guide. Email international@cie.org.uk (Subject: To Education Division: Excellence in Bilingual Education).

For further information about University of Cambridge International Examinations and bilingual education, visit: www.cie.org.uk.

Foreword

There have been many studies on different aspects of bilingual education covering linguistics, psycholinguistics, sociology, pedagogy, methodology and testing. But this is the first work devoted to the organisational aspects of a bilingual programme from the perspective of school headteachers or principals. These people are key stakeholders in the development of a successful approach to education provision, since a bilingual programme will stand or fall on the commitment of the central leading figure in a given school. This very welcome addition to the literature on bilingual education provides clear-cut, highly readable insights for those at the centre of a process involving many strands. The guide, aimed at busy practitioners, is concise and pragmatic in a user-friendly way, though based on a deep knowledge of the professional literature as well as experience of good practice in many different contexts.

Central to the conception of this slim and handy guide are the major stakeholders, who are brought together in an integrated, cohesive team as seen from a managerial perspective; this is what makes the work original. Principals, teachers, students, parents must share the aims of a common goal where two or more distinct languages form the foundation of a process seen as a long-term commitment. Such programmes cannot succeed if based on tactics and strategies built upon hit-and miss-improvisation. Unfortunately, this has often been the case when innovative bilingual forms of education have been embarked upon, and this has led to complex problems and difficult decisions when those issues that were not thought through beforehand present themselves. To help predict potential pitfalls or unexpected complications, this guide includes the 'do' and 'don't do' type of advice, based not on abstract opinion but on experience from both research and practice. There are also clear definitions and guidelines about the different types of bilingual provision that may be introduced, depending on context, outside constraints that a school must respond to but may have no power to control, and ultimate outcome goals.

Although aimed primarily at principals, and with a strong emphasis on the initial launching of some form of bilingual schooling, whether it goes under the name of CLIL (Content and Language Integrated Learning), immersion or simply bilingual education, whether it is a modest or a more intensive form of dual language provision across the curriculum, the book is of use to all stakeholders involved in producing a viable school entity. And although it focuses on how to initiate a bilingual form of education, it contains many useful insights for those already in the field: principals, teachers and parents, who can get some reassurance about what they have already embarked upon, and perhaps some answers to questions they had not addressed or that may still arise somewhere down the line. In short, this is a useful book for a large community of educators.

HUGO BAETENS BEARDSMORE
Vrije Universiteit Brussel & Université Libre de Bruxelles, and
Royal Academy for Overseas Sciences, Belgium

Preface

This guide summarises key factors for consideration during the development of bilingual education programmes. It is organised under the main headings shown in the plan below, and addresses, among others, the issues listed there.

INTRODUCTION

- key terms
- benefits of bilingualism
- benefits for the school
- programming options
- early versus late start
- research findings

PLANNING AND PARTNERS

- preparations
- admissions policy
- working with stakeholders
- managing change
- long-term planning
- monitoring and evaluation

LEADERSHIP

- instructional leadership
- language of science
- Bilingual Education Continuum
- CLIL essentials
- assessment for learning
- learning communities versus pseudo-communities
- school unity
- working with government
- media relations

STUDENTS

- supporting and retaining students
- addressing gender issues

TEACHERS

- needed competences
- finding new teachers
- keeping teachers
- professional development
- assistant teachers

PARENTS

- gaining support
- addressing concerns
- supporting parents
- involving non-programme parents

The guide also incorporates the personal perspectives of several principals and other leaders/managers of bilingual programmes in Africa, Asia, Europe, the Middle East and South America. Teachers from around the world comment on what principals can do to facilitate student and teacher learning. In addition, comments from secondary school students in North America and Europe have been included.

Additive bilingual education has the potential to help students not only to become bilingual during their school years, but to develop the skills and habits required for lifelong language learning and use. Moreover, well-managed bilingual programmes help students on average and in the long term to achieve in content subjects such as Science, History or Mathematics on the same level or better than students studying in monolingual programmes.

Although bilingual sections may have been established in a school by one enthusiastic teacher with the support of an administrator, setting up and developing a sustainable bilingual section or fully bilingual school is a complex undertaking. Successful bilingual programmes are characterised by numerous partners or stakeholders working co-operatively to build effective bilingual learning environments. Strong leadership from school principals is central to leading and managing this co-operation.

People, state schools, private schools, neighbourhoods, cities, regions and countries all vary in some ways; however, they often hold much in common. This guide seeks to trace core considerations that have been known to support the development of bilingual education in diverse contexts.

The complexities of bilingual education cannot be fully disentangled from the complexities of education in general. When best practice in education is applied, student learning has been seen to rise very significantly. In other words, by applying best practice in education, more content and language can be learned. Similarly, the complexities of leading and managing a complex organisation such as a bilingual school cannot be disentangled from best practice in leadership and management in general. As bilingual education makes extra demands on students, teachers, principals and parents, it is particularly important to offer an extra measure of support to students through the use of best practice in pedagogy. Equally importantly, an extra measure of effort is required by principals to lead/manage bilingual programmes effectively. Hence, the guide incorporates some of the best practices in teaching and learning, as well as leadership and management in general, into the discussion about bilingual education.

1 Introduction

This chapter focuses on:

- defining key terms
- describing the benefits of bilingualism for individuals
- describing the benefits of bilingual education for a school
- reviewing programming options
- reviewing the advantages and disadvantages of an early start
- reviewing the advantages and disadvantages of a late start
- major research findings regarding bilingual education.

Defining key terms

Bilingual

Challenges in using the term

The term *bilingual* is used to describe both individuals and groups of people who have varying degrees, including very high or low levels, of proficiency in two or more languages. Determining what constitutes a high degree of proficiency or fluency in one language or another is difficult. Large numbers of people speak even their strongest language with varying degrees of proficiency. Even if someone is highly proficient in one type of social or academic language (or register of speech), he or she may not be proficient in other types. Furthermore, in situations where bilingualism involves two or more languages perceived as having high status, bilinguals and bilingualism are usually presented in a positive light. In contrast, if one of the languages is perceived as having low status, bilingualism and bilinguals can be perceived as problematic by those lacking in-depth knowledge of language learning.

Definition as used in this guide

The term *bilingual* describes individuals and groups of people who use two or more languages for inter-cultural communication in varying contexts. In a bilingual education context, a bilingual is a student who is meeting curriculum expectations in those subjects taught either primarily through the first language (L1) or primarily through the second language (L2). This implies that students are also 'biliterate', having the ability to read and write in two or more languages at an age-appropriate level.

Bilingual education

Challenges in using the term

The term *bilingual education* is used by some people to refer to those programmes that support bilingualism, and by others, to those programmes that undermine bilingualism (additive versus subtractive bilingualism).[1] In some regions, programmes that teach immigrant children primarily through the societally dominant language are referred to as *bilingual education* despite the fact that these programmes may in the long term suppress the students' L1 in favour of the dominant language (subtractive bilingualism). The same is the case in some countries with numerous language groups where a former colonial language or a regional *lingua franca* is the dominant language of instruction, whilst the languages of various other ethnic groups are used to a lesser degree, or not used at all, as a medium of instruction. Cultural contexts vary, as do the challenges various societies face in delivering bilingual education. Bilingual education has in some regions become for many people such a misunderstood and negative concept that proponents of additive bilingual education have rebranded the concept using a new term such as 'dual language education', simply in order to avoid the negativity associated with the previously used term.

Definition as used in this guide

Bilingual education supports individuals in becoming and remaining bilingual (additive bilingualism). At least two languages are used to teach different content subjects such as Mathematics or History throughout the final if not all the years of school life. Bilingual education supports students in developing:

- age-appropriate levels of L1 competence in reading, writing, speaking and listening
- age-appropriate levels of advanced proficiency in L2 reading, writing, speaking and listening

[1] See the work of Wallace Lambert.

- grade-appropriate[2] levels of academic achievement in non-language school subjects, such as Mathematics and Science, taught primarily through the L2 and in those taught primarily through the L1
- an understanding and appreciation of the L1 and L2 cultures
- the capacity for and interest in inter-cultural communication
- the cognitive and social skills and habits required for success in an ever-changing world.

Note: Although the above definition constitutes a high expectation, it does not imply that lesser forms of bilingual education should be rejected. Instead, it is proposed that societies and their stakeholders work towards improving the provision of quality bilingual education in a manner that respects the linguistic rights and needs of all language groups.

 Personal perspective

Navigating diversity

Ejigayehu Zewdie works as a Project Manager at the British Council in Ethiopia. She recounts some of the challenges of developing additive bilingual education programmes in her national context:

> Twenty-one regional languages (in addition to the official language, Amharic) are used as media of instruction at the primary level, and this in a country where some 90 regional languages are spoken. In Ethiopia there is a lack of teachers able to teach in regional languages and a lack of teaching materials (for some regional languages the first step was the adoption of a script for writing them). In some regions and areas there are schools that have groups of children who speak different languages at home, which raises the challenge of defining which of the children's first languages should be used as a medium of instruction.

CLIL

Challenges in using the term

CLIL (Content and Language Integrated Learning) programmes are used to refer to a wide range of programmes from those that use the L2 for teaching one short content module or one content subject such as History or Science, to those programmes that use the L2 for teaching half or more of the curriculum.

---

[2]A grade is a synonym for a particular academic year, e.g. Grade 1 or Year 1.

Thus, descriptions of context take on a particular importance when comparing conclusions from various CLIL research studies.

Definition as used in this guide

CLIL is a dual-focused teaching and learning approach in which an additional language or two is used in content classes for promoting both content mastery and language acquisition to pre-defined levels. In addition, the goals listed under *bilingual education* also apply to CLIL. Thus, CLIL seeks additive bilingualism.

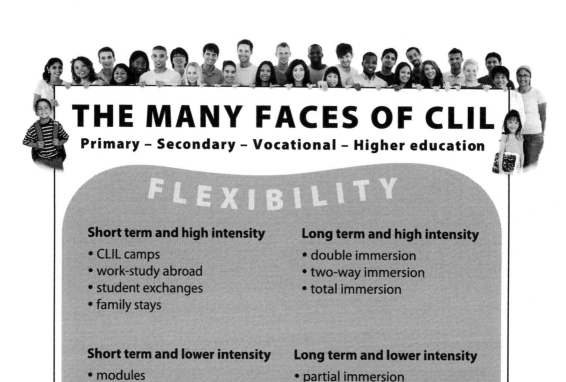

THE MANY FACES OF CLIL
Primary – Secondary – Vocational – Higher education

FLEXIBILITY

Short term and high intensity
- CLIL camps
- work-study abroad
- student exchanges
- family stays

Long term and high intensity
- double immersion
- two-way immersion
- total immersion

Short term and lower intensity
- modules
- international projects
- local projects

Long term and lower intensity
- partial immersion
- several content subjects
- one content subject

L1 (first language)

Challenges in using the term

With increased migration of people within and across regions and nations, many parts of the world are becoming more linguistically mixed and complex. With regard to language, it is increasingly difficult to use one term that applies broadly to a whole society. Furthermore, the term *L1* raises issues of identification (self, others, government bodies); levels of competence; frequency and extent of use and non-use; cultural and linguistic affiliation; power; and citizenship; all of which add further layers of meaning to the concept of *L1*.

Definition as used in this guide

The term *L1* refers to a student's first acquired and strongest language. For simplicity's sake, when referring to a situation in general, it is assumed that the L1 is also the society's numerically dominant language.[3] At the same time, it is recognised that for individual students from immigrant or minority backgrounds the L1 can be their second (L2) or even third language (L3).

L2 (second language)

Challenges in using the term

The same challenges apply to the use of the term *L2* as is the case for *L1*.

Definition as used in this guide

The term *L2* refers to a student's second language. For simplicity's sake, in this guide *L2* refers to an additional language (in addition to the L1) that is used as a medium of instruction. At the same time, it is recognised that for individual students from immigrant or minority backgrounds, the L2 can be their third (L3) or even fourth (L4) language.

Mother tongue

Challenges in using the term

In and across different contexts, the term *mother tongue* is open to a wide range of interpretations on a personal, state and international level. Some people have one mother tongue, another father tongue, and possibly a third grandparent tongue. In other environments, some children may first learn a societally dominant language, and only later as an adult learn what in more natural, tolerant or supportive circumstances would have been their mother tongue.

---

[3] In some circumstances, this is not the case. For example, in some African countries, minority speakers outnumber native speakers of the politically dominant and official language(s). Examples can be found from other continents.

Definition as used in this guide

Mother tongue is the first and primary language through which a child is initially socialised by his or her parent(s) or guardian(s). It is recognised that a child may be socialised more or less equally through two languages at one time.

Principal

A *principal* is the primary leader and manager of a school. He or she is in charge of all school staff and operations. In some countries she or he is referred to, among other titles, as the school director, headteacher or headmistress/headmaster.

Stakeholder

A *stakeholder* is any person, group or organisation that can be affected by the school's bilingual programme or that can affect the programme. Thus, a stakeholder is any person, group or organisation that can support and work with the school to build the programme or that can feel threatened by and work against the programme.

Describing the benefits of bilingualism for individuals

All of the potential benefits of bilingualism are too numerous to list in this guide. They are tied to such diverse fields as culture, economics, personal relations, health, international relations, language awareness, marketing, national security, social cohesion, trade, travel and tourism. The following sections describe some of the potential benefits for the individual, and by extension for society.

Increased mental processing capacity

Bilinguals may be better at processing a larger number of cognitive demands in a shorter timeframe. They may be able to handle more tasks at once.

Greater control over information processing

It is thought that bilingual individuals can ignore irrelevant information more easily than monolinguals when they are working on a given task. In the information-rich world of today, it is valuable to be able to determine which information is worthy of attention and which is not. In order to solve a problem effectively one needs to use relevant information and ignore the irrelevant. It is important not to allow irrelevant information to inhibit thinking. Thus, the improved ability of bilingual individuals to ignore irrelevant stimuli can contribute towards effective thinking and decision-making.

Improved memory

It is thought that the bilingual mind has superior episodic and semantic memory when compared to the monolingual. Episodic memory, as its name suggests, is about episodes or events and includes information about such elements as time, place, feelings and activities. Semantic memory includes general knowledge about, for example, ideas, facts and problem-solving. Improved memory should allow learners to work with greater amounts of information while expanding their understanding and knowledge-base, thereby improving learning in general.

Greater metalinguistic awareness

A bilingual mind draws on its metalinguistic awareness (awareness of the component parts and nature of language) to understand that words can have more than one meaning, or vary in their scope of meaning from language to language. Bilinguals are more likely to identify ambiguity in communication as they seek precision in the meaning not just of words, but of underlying concepts. This can help them to solve word problems in Mathematics or contribute to greater sensitivity in interpersonal communication.

Increased mental flexibility

Bilingual children may have earlier access to a wider range of interpretations of information than monolinguals. This offers the potential for greater cognitive flexibility. Flexibility is considered an important skill in ensuring personal happiness and an important characteristic sought after by employers.

Improved health

The knowledge of more than one language is thought to slow down mental decline by two to four years as a person ages. This may be due to the more complex neural circuitry of bilingual individuals, which could be compared to the workings of a national electric power grid: the more complex the grid, the more options are available to bypass a failing part of the circuitry and maintain power to the system as a whole.[4]

Improved inter-cultural skills

Bilingual secondary school, college and university graduates are likely to have an advantage in benefiting from international communication, mobility, perspectives and discoveries. Moreover, as it is thought that bilinguals have improved cross-cultural skills, they may be well placed, provided they have the other requisite skills, to undertake the cross-cultural communication which is necessary in addressing the complicated cross-boundary issues that have important consequences for all nations and the world at large – pollution, war, terrorism, migration and contagious diseases.

[4]See the work of Ellen Bialystok and her colleagues.

Increased opportunities for trade

Having a common language increases opportunities for international trade and thus trade flows. Equally, a lack of language and cultural skills is thought to lead to lost opportunities. It has been estimated from business surveys that in Europe, for example, billions of euros and tens of thousands of potential jobs per year are lost because of a lack of language and cultural skills.

Increased income

In situations where societies value two or more specific languages, bilinguals can earn more and have access to more job opportunities than monolinguals. However, the degree of economic gain from bilingualism for individuals varies according to region, nation, gender, sphere and level of employment, and depends on the value placed by a society on the language(s). Many employers seek high levels of proficiency in the L2. However, even limited L2 knowledge can bring considerable financial benefit in such areas as tourism.

Describing the benefits of bilingual education for a school

Added value for students and parents

Because additive bilingual programmes seek to deliver on the same academic goals as regular schools and help students to become bilingual, they can create extra value for parents and students. Both groups see that they will lose nothing through bilingual education and stand to gain an extra language. Moreover, an intellectually rigorous programme fosters increased learning in general. Finally, parents are likely to associate the potential benefits of bilingualism with the school.

A motor for reform

Establishing a bilingual programme requires a school to revisit its mission and vision statements, its pedagogical and management practices, its strategic plan and stakeholder relations. If this is done in a stakeholder-inclusive manner, current understandings are discussed and stakeholders take part in joint learning initiatives. Constructive discussions and joint learning opportunities can translate into improved programming. This in turn is likely to lead to improved student learning.

Protection against declining enrolment

The popularity of these programmes helps a school to keep students and staff in times of declining enrolment.

Increased number of visitors and exchanges

Bilingual schools draw additional attention. Although this needs to be carefully managed, increased contact and exchanges constitute new learning opportunities for students and staff.

Increased student and staff motivation

The rapid pace at which students learn the L2 in the bilingual programme is motivating for both students and staff.

Increased access to learning and teaching resources

By using two languages of instruction, a school exponentially increases the number of teaching and learning resources available to staff and students.

Reviewing programming options

Researchers have identified hundreds of different models or variations of additive bilingual education.[5] Broadly speaking, these can be grouped as: one-way immersion programmes (including double immersion); CLIL (Content and Language Integrated Learning) programmes; and two-way immersion (dual language) programmes.

One-way immersion and CLIL

One-way immersion and CLIL programmes use two or more languages primarily separately in different content classes as the medium of instruction for content subjects such as Mathematics or Geography. Immersion programmes involve several years of a child's/young person's education and at least 50% of teaching/learning time is devoted to learning through the L2. Some people also refer to these as CLIL programmes, whilst others see CLIL programmes as offering only one or a few subjects through the medium of the L2 or L3 during one school term or over several academic years. CLIL initiatives distinguish themselves through the flexibility of the approach. In immersion and CLIL programmes one language is usually the society's dominant language, and the other is perceived as having high status.

[5]For a more thorough overview of these programming options and the many nuances involved in interpreting research results and in managing the delivery of bilingual education, see the work of Hugo Baetens Beardsmore, Colin Baker, Jasone Cenoz, Do Coyle, Ofelia García, Fred Genesee, Nancy Hornberger, Guangwei Hu, Keith Johnson, Sharon Lapkin, Kathryn Lindholm-Leary, Roy Lyster, David Marsh and Merrill Swain.

Double immersion

Double immersion is an exceptional form of one-way immersion. In double immersion students study just under half of the curriculum through one language that is not their L1, and just under half of the curriculum through another language which is also not their L1 (e.g. an English-speaking child in an English-speaking neighbourhood studying an equal number of subjects through Hebrew and French). A small portion of the curriculum is delivered through the L1.

Usually, one-way immersion programmes are divided into three broad categories:

- early immersion
- delayed or middle immersion
- late immersion.

Early immersion

Early immersion programmes begin in kindergarten (at ages 4, 5 and/or 6)[6], or in Grade 1 (Year 1) when children are 6 or 7 years of age. Two primary forms of early immersion are most common – early total immersion and early partial immersion. In **early total immersion** programmes, all or almost all instruction during the initial years is provided through the L2. In Grade 3, the L1 is introduced as a subject. From Grade 4 onwards, subjects are increasingly taught through the L1. By Grade 6 (beginning at age 11 or 12), 50% of instructional time is used for teaching/learning through the L2 and 50% through the L1. In **early partial immersion** two languages are used for instruction from the start of schooling, for 50% of instructional time each.

Delayed or middle immersion

Delayed or middle immersion usually begins in Grade 4 (at age 9 or 10) or Grade 5 (at age 10 or 11). Prior to programme entry, students have usually received 30–60 minutes daily of L2 instruction from Grade 1 onwards. In Grades 4–6, they receive about 50–60% of instruction through the L2. The percentage of time allotted to teaching through the L2 often drops to 50% or less in the following grades.

Late immersion

In late immersion, students study the L2 as a second language from Grades 1 to 6 for 30–60 minutes a day. In Grade 7 (beginning at age 12 or 13) and Grade 8, 80% of instruction is delivered through the L2 and 20% through the L1. In Grades 9–11, approximately 45% of instruction is delivered through the L2 and 55% through the L1.

[6]The age at which students begin school in some countries may not be aligned with the above models.

In the above types of immersion programmes, languages are kept relatively separate with a given subject taught primarily either through the L1 or the L2.

Two-way immersion

In two-way immersion (dual language) programmes, approximately half of the students speak the society's dominant language as an L1, whilst the other half speaks one and the same minority language as an L1. Normally, half of the school curriculum is taught through one language and half through the other. For example, in the United States there are Spanish–English, Korean–English and Putonghua–English two-way immersion programmes. These programmes give students regular contact with native speakers of the additional language they are learning, and thus facilitate cross-cultural contact, co-operation and learning. They help equalise the power-base of the two language groups, as each has expertise that can benefit the other. However, the power of English in the United States has been such that some schools have chosen for a few years to use the additional language as opposed to English for a greater percentage of teaching/learning time per day to counterbalance the reality that students are often surrounded by English outside school. This can be considered a conscious effort to give both languages equal status.

Goals in immersion and CLIL

One-way and two-way (dual language) immersion and CLIL initiatives generally seek to achieve the goals listed on pages 2–3 regarding bilingual education. These goals stress the additive nature of bilingual education and address the concerns of the majority of parents who wish to ensure that children in these programmes are academically successful, that they learn as much content as students in regular L1 programmes, that they develop L2 proficiency, and that their L1 continues to develop as if the students were in a regular L1 programme.

Immersion and CLIL are both content- and language-integrated approaches. These initiatives use the standard regional or national curriculum or have received the right to use an internationally recognised high-status curriculum. In primary school, students often enter these programmes with little or no L2 proficiency. In later grades/years students usually have a working knowledge of the language prior to programme entry. The L2 is acquired primarily through education, although in contexts where the L2 is very much present in the community, considerable out-of-school learning can take place. The same can be the case with schools that foster regular contact and communication with L2 speakers. The classroom operates within the local cultural context, and makes links to both the L2 and L1 cultures. In addition to teaching content classes through both the L1 and the L2, language classes are provided in both the L1 and the L2.

Reviewing the advantages and disadvantages of an early start

In schools seeking to support students in developing additive bilingualism including biliteracy, starting to learn several or almost all subjects through the L2 in kindergarten or in the early grades of primary school can have the following advantages, disadvantages, and resource implications.[7]

Advantages of an early start

- Young learners have a natural facility to acquire new languages.
- The student-centred, activity-based, experiential approaches commonly used in primary education are highly suitable for L2 learning.
- Young learners will develop a solid foundation in the L2 that can set them on a road of continuous L2 learning, preparing them for further studies through the L2 and an L3.
- Students can transfer L2 literacy skills to reading and writing in the L1 and L3.
- Students can use both the L2 and the L1 to do research.
- Students may develop a bilingual and possibly bicultural frame of mind.
- Initially, only class teachers who teach all subjects are required. Class teachers are natural integrators of subjects and of content and language, which is a key methodological practice fostering student learning in these programmes.
- A school or education system that launches a programme in Grade 1 has time to build skills among teaching staff as students move one grade at a time through primary and secondary school.

Cross-language transfer of skills

The transfer of L1 skills to the L2 (or vice versa) applies first and foremost to alphabetic languages (based on phonemes e.g. Spanish) and to syllabary languages (based on syllables e.g. Japanese). The back and forth transfer of literacy skills between a logographic language (based on morphemes and words) such as Putonghua (Chinese) and an alphabetic language such as English requires more research. Although it is thought that some transfer of some skills can occur, teachers working to develop biliteracy in both an alphabetic language and a logographic language likely have to give greater attention to developing literacy skills in both languages. (See the work of Fred Jyun-gwang Chen; Min Wang, Keiko Kodab and Charles A. Perfetti; and Min Wang, Charles A. Perfetti and Ying Liu.)

[7]This section builds on a 2010 consultancy report by Genesee and Mehisto.

Additive/strong bilingual education

Additive/strong bilingual education programmes have different L1:L2 balances at different stages, but both L1 & L2 are used as a medium of instruction during later years.

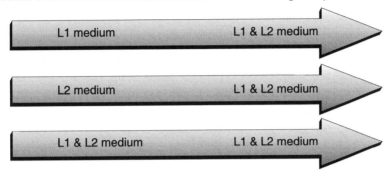

Educators largely separate the L1 & L2 by teaching a given subject primarily through one or the other language. However, educators take into account that both the L1 & L2 are *dynamic* whilst also continually interacting in the learner's mind. This invites the judicious use of the L1 by teachers teaching through the L2 and vice versa.

Additive/strong bilingual education can include an *L3*. It can also support immigrant communities in reinforcing their children's use of their communities' languages. It can support these students in drawing on their *L1* in the learning of other languages and content.

Additive/ strong bilingual education can be *recursive* in nature. In such circumstances communities revitalise their ancestral language (see the work of Ofelia García).

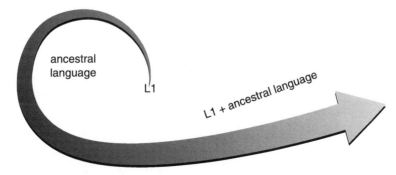

Disadvantages of an early start

- Some parents are uncomfortable having a young child learning through an L2.
- Teachers and learning resources would need to be available from the early years of schooling up to a student's graduation from secondary or vocational school.
- Large numbers of teachers teaching through the L1 may be left without employment and may undermine the programme.
- Some parents, teachers, government officials and politicians may fear that the L1 might be negatively affected (in additive bilingual contexts this is normally not the case).

Support and resource implications of an early start

The following are required:

Parents

- a sufficient number of parents choosing and supporting bilingual education
- advice and possibly some training on how to support children learning through an L2

Leadership/management

- a policy decision within a school or at a higher level
- leadership and support from education authorities
- school administrators and support staff who understand and know how to plan for and support the L2 programme
- sufficient numbers of principals who understand the leadership and management implications of running a bilingual programme

Staffing

- sufficient numbers of primary-level teachers who are trained to teach subjects through the L2, and who believe that bilingual education is suitable for a wide range of students

Training

- sufficient numbers of qualified trainers and mentors who can support teacher professional development
- professional development programmes (including curricula and materials)
- teacher-training institutions with a pre-service programme for teaching content subjects through an L2

Learning materials

- high-quality learning materials in different content areas such as Mathematics and Science that are appropriate for students learning those subjects through the L2.

Reviewing the advantages and disadvantages of a late start

In schools seeking to support students in developing additive bilingualism including biliteracy, starting to learn several subjects (or for a few years almost all subjects) through the L2 in the later grades of primary school or in the early grades of secondary school can have the following advantages, disadvantages and resource implications.

Advantages of a late start

- A late start can be as effective in helping students to develop L2 proficiency as an early start, if sufficient quality L2 input and output opportunities are provided for several years.
- A late start is more easily accepted by those parents who are concerned about early-years L1 development.
- Students can transfer L1 literacy skills to the learning of the L2 and to learning through the L2.
- Concentrating L2 instruction into later years will require fewer teachers proficient in the L2, less learning-materials development and purchasing, and fewer principals who are trained to lead and manage bilingual programmes.
- Older learners are generally more effective learners than young children.
- Older students can be more motivated learners as they may better understand the value of the L2.

Disadvantages of a late start

- The first few months of learning through the L2 are, according to teachers, difficult for older students.
- The first year may require considerably more work from students and the L2 programme will compete for space and attention with existing priorities in the students' lives.
- High-achieving students may be more likely to choose the programme and the programme may become elitist, undermining regular programming.
- Some of the potential inter-cultural benefits of an early start may be lost.
- Some parents, government officials and politicians may prefer an early start.

- Secondary school content teachers are generally not in the habit of integrating several subjects, nor have they usually been trained to teach language or to integrate content and language.
- Secondary school content teachers have generally not been trained as language teachers and may find it difficult to distinguish between content and language whilst assessing students' work.
- It may be difficult to find sufficient numbers of content teachers who are proficient in the L2 and a desire for programming may lead to pressure from any number of stakeholders to proceed with unqualified staff.
- Parents, students, government officials and politicians may be concerned that learning through the L2 will affect students' grades (this is usually only the case for the first few months of these programmes).
- There is a lack of learning materials that present challenging concepts whilst using language that is appropriate for L2 learners.

Support and resource implications of a late start

The following are required:

Parents and students

- parents and students who understand and believe in the merits and possibilities offered by a bilingual programme (older students are more likely to resist programming than younger students)

Management/leadership

- a policy decision within a school or at a higher level
- leadership and support from education authorities
- school principals and other staff who understand and know how to plan for and support the L2 programme
- a rich L2 language-teaching curriculum and programme in the early years that prepares students to learn content through the L2 in later years
- the teaching of some short modules through the L2 in the early years to prepare the way for teaching content through the L2 in later years
- an enhanced L2 language curriculum that supports the learning of academic language and concepts from content classes
- organised and well-structured opportunities for contact and communication with speakers of the L2

Teachers

- sufficient numbers of qualified teachers for teaching content subjects through the L2

- co-operation between content and language teachers
- sufficient numbers of language teachers in the early years who have been trained to prepare students for learning content through the L2

Trainers

- sufficient numbers of qualified trainers and mentors who can support the professional development of teachers
- professional development programmes (including curricula and materials)
- teacher-training institutions with pre- and in-service programmes for teaching content through an L2

Learning materials

- high-quality learning materials in different content areas such as Mathematics and Geography that are appropriate for learning those subjects through the L2
- enriched language learning materials that support the learning of academic language and concepts from content classes.

 Personal perspective

Thoughts about an Arab–English bilingual programme

Al Monshateh Dira, principal of Ahmad Bin Majid Private School in Oman, suggests:

> Sound knowledge of the L1 (Arabic) is essential to make steady progress in learning English. By starting to teach through English early, children can rely on their natural ability to learn languages quickly. It is easier to learn an L2 at this stage. However, it is **important to continue to teach through Arabic** also. Teaching phonics has helped our students learn both Arabic and English. The **L1 and L2 extra-curricular programmes** are as important as the academic ones.
>
> Study materials should be selected with care to deepen the students' understanding of Arabic culture. Our school promotes exchange programmes, so students have opportunities to communicate with young people in other countries. This builds global understanding and helps our students to better understand and feel pride in their own culture. Bilingual education helps students to think globally in addition to locally, helping them compete in the labour market.
>
> We provide **extra support** to those students who may be struggling with their L1, L2 and/or the learning of content.

Major research findings regarding bilingual education (by Fred Genesee, McGill University)

There have been many extensive and systematic evaluations of bilingual programmes around the world. These evaluations have produced information that is invaluable for school principals because they provide a scientific, empirical basis for programme development, implementation and further evaluation. This section summarises important findings from evaluations of bilingual education from various centres around the world. These findings pertain to students in bilingual programmes who are members of the **majority language** and culture group of the larger national community in which they live and are educated; for example, Spanish-speaking students in English immersion/bilingual programmes in Madrid or English-speaking students in French immersion programmes in the UK. They do not necessarily describe what would happen in programmes for minority-language students in bilingual education, for example Welsh-speaking students in the UK or Basque-speaking students in Spanish bilingual programmes.

First major finding: L1 proficiency

Majority-language students in bilingual programmes attain the same levels of proficiency in reading, writing, speaking and listening in their L1 as similar students being educated entirely in the L1. Students in bilingual programmes also attain the same levels of achievement in academic domains, such as Mathematics and Science, as similar majority-language students in L1 programmes even though they have been taught these academic subjects in their L2. Moreover, there is no consistent relationship in the long run between how much instruction in and through the L1 students receive and their proficiency in their L1. That is to say, majority-language students with less exposure to the L1 do not achieve at lower levels of proficiency in the L1 than students with more exposure to the L1.

Implication: Bilingual education is not a zero-sum game whereby achievement in the L2 detracts from students' L1 development. Thus, school principals do not need to worry that students' L1 development or academic achievement will suffer as a result of education in two languages. However, principals need to help teachers and parents to minimise unjustified concerns regarding L1 development through discussions that are informed by research evidence.

Second major finding: L2 proficiency

Students in bilingual programmes achieve significantly higher levels of functional proficiency in the L2 than students who receive conventional foreign/second language instruction, and they are able to pursue academic studies in the L2 without difficulty. Students' proficiency in the L2 is generally related to the amount of instruction they have in and through the L2 – students in total immersion outperform students in partial immersion, for example. Thus, more exposure to the L2 usually results in greater proficiency without reducing students' L1 competence.

Implication: Schools should offer substantial, quality exposure to the second language to ensure maximum development of that language.

Third major finding: L2 competence levels

Notwithstanding evidence that students in bilingual programmes attain very advanced levels of functional proficiency in the L2, they seldom achieve native-like levels of competence in the language. Research shows that students' L2 proficiency can be enhanced if they have opportunities to learn and use that language outside school and if the curriculum provides systematic and focused instruction in areas of the L2 that they have trouble acquiring (such as verb tenses, use of prepositions and pronouns). (See Lyster 2007 for further readings.)[8]

Implication: Principals can support staff in planning for and creating well-structured opportunities for students to communicate, and to network in the long term, with speakers of the L2. In addition, content teachers require ongoing professional-development opportunities to support students in increasing their academic language proficiency. Staff benefit from principals who maintain a focus on these issues.

Fourth major finding: Suitability for a wide range of learners

Bilingual programmes are suitable for majority-language students with a wide range of learner characteristics, including students who are often at risk for low academic achievement. This includes students from disadvantaged socio-economic backgrounds, students with low levels of academic or general intellectual ability, and students with poorly developed L1 language skills. These students achieve the same levels of proficiency in their L1 and in academic domains in immersion programmes as similarly disadvantaged students in L1 language programmes. At the same time, they achieve significantly higher levels of proficiency in the L2 than students who receive traditional foreign/second language instruction.

Implication: Principals can develop programmes that are equitable and open to students with diverse learning competencies. They can work to build a school ethos that demonstrates a belief in the capacity of all students to succeed. 'Elite' programmes can be vulnerable to criticisms, such as: 'they undermine other programmes or schools'; making bilingual programmes accessible to all students avoids such criticisms.

[8]Roy Lyster (2007). *Learning and Teaching Languages through Content: A Counterbalanced Approach.* Amsterdam: John Benjamins.

Fifth major finding: Languages from different-language families

Bilingual programmes for majority-language students are equally effective with languages from different-language families; for example, English immersion for Japanese-speaking students in Japan; Estonian immersion for Russian-speaking students in Estonia; and Hebrew immersion for English-speaking students in Canada.

Implication: School principals can be equally confident that bilingual education can work in their community regardless of the specific characteristics of the languages involved.

Sixth major finding: Appreciation and understanding of L1 culture

Majority-language students in bilingual programmes develop the same appreciation and understanding of their L1 culture and community as students in L1 programmes. At the same time, depending on the nature of the curriculum, they can also develop greater understanding and appreciation of the L2 culture.

Implication: Bilingual education can be a useful tool for promoting inter-cultural understanding, tolerance and appreciation. The extent to which a programme achieves this depends on how much cultural content is included in the curriculum and how many well-structured opportunities are created for inter-cultural communication.

2 Planning and partners

This chapter focuses on:

- preparing for the launch of bilingual education
- developing an admissions policy
- determining and working with stakeholders
- managing change
- planning in the long term
- monitoring and evaluation.

Preparing for the launch of bilingual education

Initiating a bilingual programme is the start of a multi-year change process. As students move from year to year (grade to grade) through the programme, this will have an impact on staffing, professional development needs, purchasing of learning materials for classrooms and the school library, and on the whole school culture, which will be feeling the ever-increasing presence of the bilingual programme.

To be prepared for the change process, principals and their deputies are well advised to read about bilingual programme development, and to meet with people who have managed a bilingual school. It is helpful if those teachers who are expected to be involved in the launch of the programme do the same.

Being knowledgeable about bilingual programme methodology, planning implications and research on student achievement is often essential in gaining the support of local education authorities. In addition, a critical mass of people in the school's management and teaching team and on the board of governors need to support the idea. Teachers are probably concerned about job security. When existing staff members assume responsibility for teaching in the bilingual programme, opposition arising from the fear of job losses is reduced. Also, a sufficient number of parents need to be interested in the proposed programme (see section on *Parents*, page 100).

Before establishing a bilingual programme, it is important to ask these questions:

- **What are the school's strengths and weaknesses?** Parents will first and foremost seek a strong school that delivers a quality education, is supportive of students and has a reputation for co-operating with parents.

- **Are there enough students to allow for a class to be formed?** Several schools prefer to start with large classes to allow for the possibility of attrition. When students leave the bilingual programme, they are normally not replaced unless new students apply who have been in a similar programme and/or have the required level of language. If considerable attrition takes place, it can become very expensive to maintain programming. If not all parents are interested in the bilingual programme, a school can offer a two-track system (bilingual and regular monolingual programme). However, a two-track system may experience greater student attrition rates in the bilingual programme than is the case in schools offering only a bilingual programme.

- **Are there provisions in place for the school to reach out to the wider community?** As there is a commonly held false perception that bilingual education is suitable only for gifted children, many parents may never attend an information meeting offered by a bilingual school. Bilingual schools should try to reach out to the wider community by attending prenatal classes, community events, and nursery school and kindergarten parent meetings to provide information and an opportunity for discussion about bilingual education.

- **Is there enough space in the school to allow for increased enrolment?** Bilingual schools can become magnets, drawing students from outside the school's immediate area. However, if a programme expands rapidly, drawing many high-performing students from other schools, opposition to it will grow. Moreover, this can lead to the weakening of other schools, which would not be in the community's interest.

- **Are the classrooms large enough?** Space is required for group and pair work which are central to learning in bilingual education. In addition, for the early years, it is helpful if there is enough space to create small learning centres and to have a carpeted area where the whole class can sit on the floor.

- **Can the classrooms where the L2 is used be located away from noisy areas such as gymnasiums?** Learning through an additional language is highly dependent on hearing.

- **Are there currently enough qualified teachers who are prepared to teach through the L2 and who are willing to learn about best teaching/learning practices in bilingual education?** Further, is there a pool of qualified potential teachers to meet future needs?
- **Is there easy access to the school?** A bilingual school may draw students from a larger area than its own neighbourhood. Sufficient transport options need to be available. More space may be required for parking and for dropping students off at the school. If a school creates a traffic problem, local opposition to the bilingual programme will grow.

Moreover, a school establishing a bilingual programme needs to be prepared for the following changes:

- **The school will receive many visitors.** Educational innovations such as bilingual education draw interest from the media, university researchers, university students wishing to research programme implementation, and parents of potential students, among others.
- **The school will be asked to share its expertise.** Other schools establishing similar programmes will seek advice; so will researchers, administrators and teacher trainers.
- **The school releases teachers for professional development and planning.** Teachers will need extra time for visiting other bilingual schools, for training and for planning the integration of subjects.
- **New learning materials are purchased.** L2 language materials will be needed for the classroom and the school library. In addition to typical learning materials, class sets of dictionaries will be required.
- **Strategies are in place to support students in difficulty.** Otherwise they may drop out of the programme (see pages 72–76).
- **Leadership opportunities are widely distributed.** Bilingual education is too complex for any one person to hold all the knowledge required to manage such programmes. Considerable co-operation is required among staff members and with other stakeholders. Ideally, problems and concerns are discussed openly and people determine together what additional knowledge they need to acquire in order to manage and deliver programming successfully.

Developing an admissions policy

Although some education systems automatically enrol students in bilingual programmes, others offer varying degrees of choice. Five methods are commonly used for admitting students to bilingual programmes:

- first come, first served
- a lottery

- testing
- choosing students with the highest grades
- automatic enrolment.

First come, first served

This is the most frequently chosen option, as parents generally see it as fair.
They have some level of influence, as one of them or a family friend can queue
up early on or before the first day of registration. In the case of state-financed
popular bilingual programmes, parents have been known to camp out in front
of a school for days before the start of student registration to ensure a place
for their child. To keep the peace with neighbours, schools are advised to
allow parents to spend the night inside the school. The first come, first served
option helps avoid elitism. It also means that students with special needs may
enrol in the programme, which has its own implications. For example, when
hearing-impaired students are enrolled, teachers require special training.
Hearing-impaired students are ideally already being supported in becoming
fully bilingual, developing fluency in the dominant language of society and
the corresponding sign language.[1] What will be an L2 for most of the other
students will often be an L3 for the hearing-impaired students.

Lotteries

Lotteries are used in areas where demand far outstrips availability. Although
many see this as a fair option that avoids elitism, it leaves some parents unhappy.
They have no way of influencing the process. Schools using this option go to
great lengths to ensure the lottery is transparent and open to public scrutiny.

Testing and choosing students with the highest grades

Testing and, in the case of older learners, choosing students with the highest
grades are seen as the least desirable options. It is highly questionable whether
testing of young children for their suitability for learning in a bilingual
programme is effective and whether testing instruments are fair and devoid
of cultural and socio-economic biases. Moreover, testing may discourage
certain parents and students from applying to the programme. Testing has the
potential to create elitist programmes for high-achieving students.

Elitist programmes are far more likely to suffer funding cuts, create jealousy
and distort the make-up of the regular programme in a given school or in
neighbouring schools. Moreover, such programmes exclude large segments of
the student population that have much to gain from bilingual education.

---

[1] The exact number of sign languages in the world is unknown, but is at least in the hundreds.

Testing is appropriate when schools expect students to have a certain level of proficiency in the L2 upon programme entry. It is important for those taking the test to be well informed about the type of testing they will undergo and how the test results will be evaluated. A school has to be prepared to explain and defend the validity and equitable nature of its testing instruments and procedures. Moreover, stakeholders will want to know whether students are chosen only on the basis of their test scores or whether other criteria come into play. For example, are all the students who achieve the baseline score admitted, or only those with the highest scores? Are other criteria such as recommendation letters or a child's school record taken into account, and if so, how and to what extent? Those students who do not meet the baseline for programme entry deserve advice on what they need to do in order to reach that baseline.

Automatic enrolment

The fifth option involves having automatic enrolment in the programme as a default position, with parents having to opt out of the bilingual programme or with no opt-out option being available. In these cases, it is important to make certain that parents and older students are well informed about programme goals and potential benefits. As is the case with any major education programme, provisions are made to support students with special needs. As this guide is about additive bilingual contexts, it is assumed that this option also supports students throughout their education in developing both their L1 and L2 skills and in becoming biliterate.

General considerations

Meetings with parents and students

Some schools hold individual meetings with parents and/or students to ensure that the implications of learning through the L2 are understood (see pages 100–109), and to identify any concerns or issues which may need to be addressed.

Registration forms

Although registration forms for any of the above programme entry options are not necessary, they can serve several useful purposes. For example, they can include a statement that parents (and students in the case of late entry programmes) sign. The statement can point out that it is recommended that students remain in the bilingual programme for its intended duration, and that the school seeks to co-operate with parents, expecting them to attend home–school meetings. This helps those signing to understand the serious nature of the programme and that they, too, will have to assume responsibility for its success.

Children with different L1

Children who do not speak a society's dominant language can gain benefit from being in a bilingual programme. As all students entering the programme usually do not speak the L2, this places the immigrant child in classes taught through the school's L2 on a more linguistically equal footing with the other students.

Withdrawing students

With the first four options for programme admissions, having a **policy** and process in place for withdrawing students will help to manage these difficult situations when they arise. In general, practitioners do not advise withdrawing students from bilingual programmes. A student's problems will probably not be resolved by moving to a monolingual programme. Instead, it is normally recommended that students be provided extra support/help. The extra stimulation of learning through an L2 can have a positive impact on learning in general. By leaving the programme, students may feel a sense of failure. This can undermine their motivation to learn as well as lead to behavioural problems.

A decision to withdraw a student is based on an **assessment process**. This would include assessing the appropriateness of the various strategies used to support the student. For example, was a 'learning team' formed to support the child or instead was a team first formed to justify the withdrawal? A well thought through decision to withdraw a student would take into account the student's own sense of well-being and consider the issue of future need. If a student is living in a bilingual community where she or he will be disadvantaged by not being bilingual, the decision can carry greater consequences. Students who are withdrawn from the bilingual programme need to be provided with support to make the transition to the regular monolingual programme. A transition team can be formed to make certain that this major change in the student's learning path is as smooth as possible and that the student receives the support needed to address his or her learning difficulties.

Determining and working with stakeholders

Although its main features are well researched, bilingual education always operates in a complex world of personal beliefs, assumptions, competing priorities and agendas. Schools have much to gain if their principals are able to understand, synthesise and work through divergent as well as shared individual views, while being able to influence and to support stakeholder learning, the building of a common understanding and the co-construction of change.

In other words, **good stakeholder relations** are the connective tissue that helps a school and its partners work together for the benefit of students and the community. Many of a school's internal stakeholders have well-formed opinions about bilingual education and are probably already communicating these to each other. A school's external stakeholders may have varying levels of awareness of, and be communicating to others to varying degrees about, a school's bilingual programme, or be completely unaware of it. This may influence a school's bilingual programme or represent a lost opportunity. The process of systematically identifying a school's internal and external stakeholders is a first step in **stakeholder analysis** and in managing stakeholder relations and increasing constructive stakeholder involvement. The following lists of stakeholders are very extensive. Each of these stakeholders cannot be given equal attention. A school will need to decide which ones have greater power and influence, and then decide which ones will receive what degree of attention, if any.

Internal stakeholders

In a school or a group of schools offering or wishing to offer bilingual programming, internal stakeholders comprise the following main categories of stakeholders and additional subgroups of stakeholders.

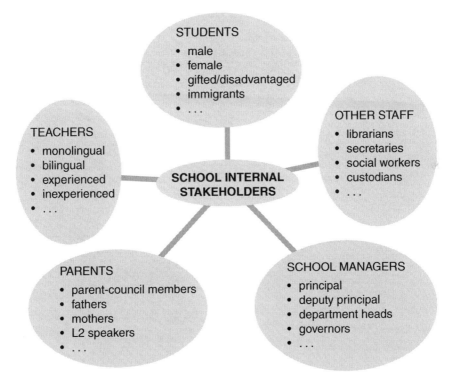

Students

Male, female, those with learning difficulties, gifted, socio-economically disadvantaged, socio-economically advantaged, primary school, secondary school, immigrants, those belonging to student associations.

Parents

Parent-council members, mothers, fathers, guardians, those who are socio-economically advantaged or disadvantaged, bilinguals, monolinguals, speakers of a regional language, non-speakers of a regional language.

Teachers

Monolinguals, bilinguals, those teaching through the L1, those teaching through the L2, those teaching through the L3, experienced, inexperienced, those opposed to bilingual programming, those supportive of bilingual education, those opposed to regional languages, leaders.

Other staff

Librarians, secretaries, psychologists, social workers, custodians, canteen workers, monolinguals, bilinguals, those supportive of bilingual programming, those opposed to bilingual programmes.

School managers

Principals, deputy principals, section or department heads, governors.

External stakeholders

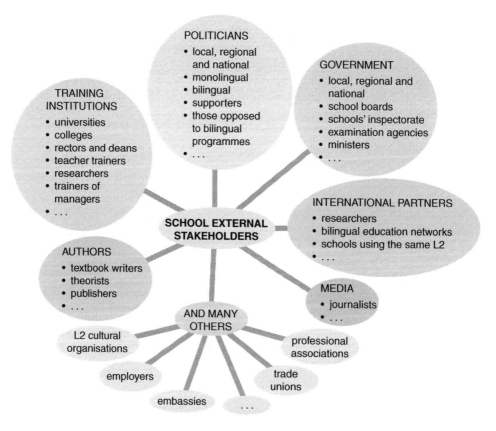

A school's or a group of schools' external stakeholders comprises:

Politicians

Local, regional, national, monolingual, bilingual, those in favour of regional languages, those against regional languages, those on committees and councils, including parliamentary committees.

Government

Local government, boards of education, an inspectorate of schools, regional and national ministries of education, culture, labour and immigration, ministerial departments, ministers, agencies administering regional or national exams, committees, councils, groups or individuals within any of these organisations.

Training institutions

Universities, teacher-training colleges, rectors, deans, teacher trainers, researchers, trainers of managers, those opposed to bilingualism, those supportive of bilingualism.

Authors

Textbook writers, creators of online resources, theorists, publishers.

Media

Journalists from radio, television or print and electronic media, those supportive of bilingual education, those opposed to bilingual education.

International partners

Educators, researchers, international bilingual education networks, schools using your school's L2 as a medium of instruction, individuals or groups that have spearheaded the successful implementation of bilingual programming.

Others

Parent associations, teacher associations and unions, student associations and unions, trade unions, employers, professional associations, embassies, L2 cultural organisations, sponsors.

Managing stakeholder relations

In undertaking a stakeholder analysis it is helpful if school staff speculate how stakeholders would answer the questions below. Afterwards, stakeholders or a representative selection of stakeholders can be surveyed to find out what they think. The following questions can serve as a **discussion framework**:

- What does each stakeholder group want or expect from the bilingual programme?
- How does each stakeholder group judge the success of the programme?

- How (at this given time) does each stakeholder group consider the programme is performing?
- How would the stakeholder group like to work with the school?

In answering the above questions, stakeholders can be encouraged to take into account school climate, school values, language teaching, teaching of non-language subjects, extra-curricular activities, and hard data such as retention rates and student achievement. It would also be wise to provide stakeholders with a one-page synopsis of the school's strategic plan.

Stakeholders often appreciate being asked for their input. They will, however, want **an overview** of the school's stakeholder analysis to which they contributed. During any feedback session with the stakeholders, it is also important for a school to discuss what it believes it needs from each stakeholder group.

If stakeholders are to take the school's intention of building a partnership seriously, the analysis of stakeholder expectations and needs will have to lead to some changes in the school's planning documents and in the way it works with students and its other stakeholders.

Managing stakeholder relations is strongly tied to the quality of **dialogue** that takes place. Several researchers point to the need for dialogue to be **open and frank, yet constructive**. It is suggested that the dialogue be focused on developing partnerships, as opposed to placating or manipulating stakeholders, or simply sharing information with them. It is easier to manage dialogue if the guidelines for the discussion process and the goals stakeholders wish to accomplish have first been jointly agreed upon. Once again, stakeholders will want to feel they have some influence over the decisions that a school makes.

Managing change

Change management is a science of its own. It explores those practices and models that can be used by an organisation to manage change more effectively. The introduction of bilingual education represents a major change for any school. Change is a 'messy' business. For instance, the well-ordered models presented in the diagram on page 31 do not necessarily operate in a linear fashion. Awareness of change-management models, principles and techniques can help principals bring greater order to the inevitably challenging but potentially energising process of establishing or renewing a bilingual education programme.

Kotter[2] details eight steps that characterise successful change initiatives: establishing a sense of urgency that is based on an authentic need; creating

[2]Kotter, J. P. (1996). *Leading Change*. Boston: Harvard Business School Press.

a guiding coalition of key stakeholders; developing strategy and vision; extensively communicating a concise vision of the change; empowering broad-based action to accomplish the vision; generating and communicating short-term wins along the road to achieving the vision; consolidating gains and producing more change; and anchoring new approaches in work culture.

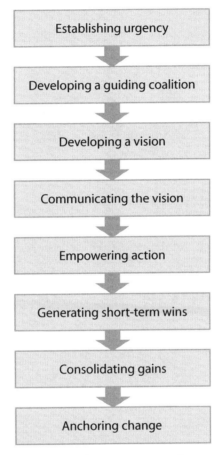

Fullan[3] proposes: maintaining a focus on moral purpose; understanding change; increasing coherence among various aspects of a planned change; relationship-building; knowledge creation and sharing; and building commitment among an organisation's internal and external members (stakeholders). (See the base of the illustration on page 32.)

Bennet and Bennet[4] suggest that professionals undertake the changes they see fit. Individuals are encouraged to manage their own learning, and to plan change by taking into account the following factors: awareness, understanding,

---

[3]Fullan, M. (2001). *Leading in a Culture of Change.* San Francisco: Jossey-Bass.
[4]Bennet, A. and Bennet, D. (2010). Organizational Learning Portfolio. *VINE* 38 (4) 378–87.

personal feelings and beliefs, ownership, empowerment and impact. This is in line with research that shows that schools that identify their own needs and plan their own changes are more likely to accomplish what they set out to do than is the case when someone from the outside identifies needs and mandates targets to be achieved.

Planning in the long term

Researchers have found a direct link between how long a principal remains at a given school and the existence of an inclusively constructed strategic plan. The strategic planning process is lengthy, but usually brings big returns. It saves time, helps avoid mistakes, and encourages a school and its stakeholders to work together in a co-ordinated manner to achieve agreed-upon goals. It can also give a sense of comfort to a principal and to school stakeholders to know that there is general agreement on what to focus on and how to move forward. Satisfaction can be gained from seeing how planning goals are met. Furthermore, once a strategic plan is in place, budget decisions, the development of work and professional development plans, the assessment of progress – to name but a few aspects of managing a school – all become easier. The following sections outline the long-term planning considerations that have been reported by principals of bilingual schools.

A strategic plan

Vision without action is daydream. Action without vision is nightmare.
— Japanese proverb

A pivotal piece

A strategic plan is a major reference-point for discussions with stakeholders, for decision-making, for creating work-plans and for school self-assessment. It is a pivotal piece in the **evaluation** of the entire school and the bilingual programme. An effective strategic plan is **short**, possibly fitting on one A4 or A3 sheet of paper. A short plan is more easily processed by all and more likely to contain a realistic number of goals.

Co-operating with stakeholders

Co-operating with stakeholders is central to identifying needs and developing a strategic plan that stakeholders will be prepared to support. Developing a plan also involves deciding on a limited number of long-term outcomes the school is seeking to achieve. To do so one would need to assess the current state of affairs in a school including student achievement; undertake the stakeholder analysis described above; and agree on the school's intended residual curriculum – what school graduates will recall and be able to use as adults.

Strategic goals/outcomes

Strategic goals or intended outcomes are **precise**. For example, instead of stating a vague goal such as 'Building stakeholder support for the bilingual programme', a more tangible outcome would be: 'School external stakeholders support the bilingual programme and contribute resources to its management, development and implementation.' This intended outcome or goal would be followed by a series of strategies for achieving the goal, one of which might be: 'Develop a communications strategy to be delivered in partnership with stakeholders.'

Similarly, instead of stating that a goal is 'to cut costs by 10%', a more focused outcome would be: 'The school will use resources 10% more effectively and increase transparency.' One related strategy might be: 'Evaluate existing resource-use with a view to maximising efficiency, effectiveness and student learning.'

The majority of a school's strategic goals/outcomes should be **tied to student learning** such as 'All students will have improved levels of content and language achievement.' A related strategy could include: 'Develop a learning-skills enhancement programme for content and language learning'.

Indicators for measuring success

By also including indicators for measuring the success of each strategic goal/outcome, the school gains an understanding of and greater control over how stakeholders will measure programme success. Effective success-indicators are usually simple, measurable, attainable and relevant and have been agreed upon by stakeholders. In work-plans indicators would also be time-bound, indicating when goals or various steps towards reaching final outcomes will be achieved.

Other long-term planning considerations

Co-operation and communication

- **An organisation or subcommittee.** Bilingual schools will have their own set of needs. To lobby authorities, principals of bilingual schools may consider establishing an organisation of their own or a subcommittee in an existing organisation. Such an organisation can agree on criteria for the evaluation (success indicators) of a bilingual programme which will make it more likely that these will be respected, and make the programme less vulnerable to stakeholder criticism. Stakeholders need access to programme research data and evaluation reports, and possibly help in interpreting this data. In any case, opportunities are required to discuss the data.
- **Neighbouring schools.** Co-operation with neighbouring schools contributes to learning, and can reduce opposition to bilingual programming from regular schools. By co-operating with other schools, a school not only learns from others, but gets a better sense of what it has accomplished.
- **Ongoing stakeholder dialogue.** Once a programme is operating successfully there is a tendency to communicate less with stakeholders, and to assume that new teachers know more than they do. It is important to maintain ongoing dialogue with stakeholders.

Language issues

Agreements are made at least every two years on **how much L1 and L2 are used** in classes that are taught primarily through either the L1 or L2. For classes taught through the L2, this usually involves agreeing on what constitutes a judicious use of the L1. For example, this could include the teacher using the L1 after an L2 explanation has failed (code-switching), having students interpret (orally translate) the occasional term from the L2 into the L1 if there is reason to suspect students are not understanding it, and having students on occasion research a topic in the L1 and report on it through the L2 (translanguaging[5]). Also, group work can at times be conducted in the L1 to foster increased

[5]See the work of Cen Williams.

student-to-student verbal interaction. This can act as a scaffold for content learning whilst supporting the learning of related L1 terms. At other times, students may be encouraged and supported in doing group work in the L2.

The agreement on language use can **vary from grade to grade.** In total early immersion, it is important at the start of a programme to build L2 skills. At this stage students may code-switch to the L1 when they do not know how to say something in the L2, at which point the teacher mirrors back that language in the L2. If at a later stage code-switching and translanguaging are being misused as a crutch, their use is restricted. For example, once students have sufficient mastery of the L2 they can be encouraged, in situations where they cannot think of a term in the L2, to use the L2 to explain their point using different words (circumlocution or paraphrasing) instead of resorting to code-switching. In addition, in classes taught through the L1 an agreement can be made to ensure terminology is also taught in the L2. It would also be important to agree on how terminology taught initially in the L2 will also be taught and used in the L1. If these agreements are not made, there will probably be large variations in expectations and in practice.

Additional language issues:

- **Other L1s.** Teachers may need professional development on how to support immigrant children in using their L1 as a resource in learning their L2 and L3. For example, students can use L1 sources to research a topic (translanguaging). Before becoming fully literate in their L2, students can write parts of a school project in their L1. Immigrant parents can benefit from information about the value of supporting their child's L1 development and strategies for doing so.

- **L3 instruction.** A decision will be required to determine when L3 instruction will be introduced and in what form, and when and if some content subjects will be taught through the L3. Bilingual schools in non-English-speaking regions that are teaching through an L2 which is not English often find that parents expect their children to also learn English. Knowledge of English is being considered in many contexts a basic skill, and the L3 (and L4) as providing a competitive edge.

- **Contact with L2 and L3 speakers.** Classroom learning inevitably leads to the acquisition of a restricted set of L2 registers of speech. Plans need to be in place to create opportunities for well-structured and safe contact and communication with L2 speakers, including in diverse contexts such as through work placements. The same is the case for the L3.

- **Sustaining interest.** If a school begins to reduce the number of classes taught through the L2 in the last years of secondary school, interest in the programme may decline, and attrition may increase.

- **University progression.** If universities do not consider bilingualism as an asset or offer the option of continued studies through the L2, interest in the programme may drop in secondary school.

Teaching and learning

- **Joint planning.** There is a greater need for teachers in bilingual schools to plan jointly for the integration of content and language and of several content subjects. Consequently, in addition to building in planning opportunities, organising professional development in the essentials of teamwork (productive and unproductive roles/behaviour, phases in group development, co-operation skills) can be helpful.
- **School curriculum.** The school curriculum will probably need to be adapted. The language-learning component in content classes can be drawn out so that content teachers have a better idea of how they can support language learning. This will assist content teachers in making intended language outcomes for content classes visible to their students. Conversely, the way language classes will support content learning can also be drawn out in the curriculum.
- **Exhibiting work.** In particular at the primary school level, schools are advised to allow walls, windows, hallways and even ceilings to be used to exhibit language and subject content, as well as student work. Subject teachers would benefit from having their own classroom, as it is too much work to develop surface areas in several classrooms.
- **Learning materials.** Learning materials are always in short supply. A school can create an intranet space where materials are well archived and shared. However, teachers can be reluctant to share materials. They will need to be consulted on what prevents them from sharing materials and what would encourage them to do so. Someone has to manage this exercise in knowledge-management. Some schools include 'sharing ideas and materials' as an agenda item for school or inter-school meetings. Sharing can be used as an evaluation criterion during performance reviews and in deciding on promotions.

Staff

(See also the section on *Teachers*, page 81.) Long-term staffing considerations include:

- **Exit plans.** These are required for teachers leaving a school, not simply to recognise them for their contribution to the school, but to help ensure that they pass on some of their experience to others.
- **Transitions.** Teachers' needs change from year to year. For example, a teacher who has successfully taught a content subject through an L2 in one grade is not

necessarily prepared to do so at a higher grade. He or she may be comfortable teaching in the L2 when concepts can be easily expressed through visuals, but may not know how to teach more abstract concepts through the L2.

- **Librarian support.** The school librarian may require support in developing L2 proficiency and in purchasing L2 books and other resources. In addition, he or she may need help in learning how to classify books according to language level. In the ideal, a librarian is also capable of guiding students in doing research through their L2.

Parents and students

Long-term parental concerns include:

- **Graduation diplomas.** Parents and eventually students will wish to know if a bilingual qualification will be indicated on the school graduation diploma or if the school will provide students with a certificate of bilingualism. In the state sector, initiating a change to diplomas can be a very lengthy process that often requires several schools to co-operate in order to raise the awareness of the appropriate authorities.

- **Continuity.** Parents will also seek assurances that the school has the teaching staff to maintain the bilingual programme through to graduation.

- **Examinations.** If the school chooses to use internationally recognised benchmark examinations, parents and older students will wish to be informed sooner rather than later of the particulars associated with sitting these examinations.

 Personal perspective

Adjusting the curriculum

Jim Johnston (British Council) supports bilingual schools in Colombia. He suggests:

Understanding the challenge

Bilingual schools are often trying to follow two curricula – the national curriculum and an international curriculum. Aligning the two curricula is something that we do to avoid duplication, fill gaps and plan effective teaching and learning.

Mapping curriculum requirements

First we compare the international and the national curricula. This helps to identify topics in the national curriculum that are not in the international curriculum, or vice versa, and to find a logical place to insert them into the bilingual programme. It helps schools plan when and in what order certain concepts will be taught.

Identifying gaps at school level

We apply international benchmark testing of students at different ages, in order to identify gaps in the existing programme. Three reasons for these gaps are: the international learning objectives may not have been included in the national curriculum, the objectives may be in the programme but were not taught, or learning did not take place effectively. Once the reasons are identified, the school is ready to take action and teachers can address the gaps.

Building a flexible sequence for learning

Sometimes topics in the international curriculum may be introduced at an earlier age than in the national curriculum. Therefore, schools may not be able to meet the objectives of the international curriculum based on the age of a given group. Here, the international curriculum may need to be adapted. The sequence of learning may have to change. This requires schools to develop a long-term plan for aligning the local and international curricula over a period of three to five years. You cannot walk into a school, flip a switch, and have it become a bilingual school. It takes hard work, perseverance and time – but in the long term it is well worth this effort.

Monitoring and evaluation

Enabling individual and group development and learning are the prime purposes of programme monitoring and evaluation. Monitoring and evaluation are less about control than they are about having reference points for and data on which to base a reasoned professional dialogue about bilingual education. Monitoring and evaluation are used for being tough on problems, not on people. Moreover, the data and the actions taken based on that data can build confidence in and support for a bilingual programme. Stakeholders expect to see and discuss data.

Key considerations

Monitoring and evaluation in bilingual programmes seek first and foremost to maintain a focus on:

- student learning of content, language, and related learning skills
- stakeholder learning about and capacity to support the bilingual programme

- the ongoing development of effective bilingual learning environments
- the achievement of the school strategic plan and subsequent work-plan targets
- programme management/leadership.

If all of the above, and other aspects of bilingual programmes listed below, are not monitored and evaluated, some of these may not receive the attention and resources they require whilst others might be overemphasised. For example, without measuring language and content learning in all classes, learning of one or the other may suffer. Without measuring student satisfaction, and the extent to which staff members co-operate, information fundamental to developing the bilingual programme will not be brought to light. Problems and opportunities first need to be identified and named. Only then is it possible to deal consciously and systematically with those problems and make the most of the opportunities. Monitoring and evaluation are essential to this process as they are tools for gathering, analysing and discussing information.

Furthermore, bilingual programmes need to gather data longitudinally over many years. This allows stakeholders to see long-term results pertaining to student achievement, stakeholder co-operation and programme management. Data about long-term results helps avoid misinterpretation of short-term results such as the significance of any initial lag in language or content learning. In particular, to avoid misinterpretations of evaluation data and to plan any necessary measures suggested by the data, opportunities are required for discussion with stakeholders.

Multiple sources

Any single evaluation can be misconceived and produce inaccurate data. Data becomes more reliable when it is generated from several sources and these different datasets are cross-checked. When different stakeholders, methods and researchers arrive at similar conclusions, data forms a more solid basis for decision-making.

Sources, frameworks and benchmarks

Principals use the following sources, frameworks and benchmarks to obtain feedback on programming:

Sources and frameworks

- one-on-one and group meetings and correspondence with students, parents, staff and/or other stakeholders
- stakeholder roundtables using an external facilitator

- anonymous surveys (anonymity guarantee must be visibly well managed)
- enrolment and retention rates (including on gender and socio-economic status)
- stakeholder analysis (see *Determining and working with stakeholders*, p 26)
- meetings with heads of sections or departments (at least once a month)
- analysis frameworks, e.g. SWOT (internal strengths and weaknesses, external opportunities and threats); STEEPLED (social, technological, economical, environmental, political, legal, ethical, demographic); Geert Hofstede's cultural dimensions (power distance, individualism, masculinity, uncertainty avoidance, long-term orientation)
- staff meetings (at least once a month)
- school walkabouts
- lesson observations
- graduates (educational and career path)
- self-reflection and assessment frameworks
- peers
- audits and inspections
- employers

Benchmarks/benchmark instruments

- strategic-plan and work-plan goals/outcomes/indicators
- key performance indicators (KPI)
- curriculum expectations/goals/outcomes
- student grades over several years
- stakeholder satisfaction levels over several years
- survey response rates
- best practice (pedagogy and management) as evidenced by research results (professional literature)
- internationally recognised examinations
- league tables
- proficiency guidelines and rating scales – for example:
  - American Council on the Teaching of Foreign Languages (ACTFL) proficiency guidelines for speaking and writing
  - Cambridge ESOL proficiency standards (see www.cambridgeesol.org.uk)
  - Centre for Applied Linguistics (CAL) Oral Proficiency Exam and Student Oral Proficiency Assessment Rating Scale (see www.cal.org for additional instruments)
  - Common European Framework of Reference for Languages

  - School-produced exemplars of written and videotaped work that has been mapped to proficiency standards
  - Teachers of English to Speakers of Other Languages (TESOL) PreK–12 English Language Proficiency Standards.

Objects of monitoring and evaluation

Many managers have been heard to say: 'You can't manage what you can't or don't measure.' Some objects of monitoring or evaluation are shown in the diagram on page 42. They cannot all be part of constant formal evaluation. However, all are worthy of evaluation at some time, whether formally or informally.

Evaluation pitfalls

- If student achievement results are over-emphasised and become the primary goal of education, the quality of education and student motivation will probably decline. People tend to value what is measured. Instead, assessment or evaluation data can be used as a valuable benchmark of school and student progress – but then the emphasis needs to shift to good pedagogy. Furthermore, the scope of what is measured needs to be wide enough to increase the likelihood that other aspects of learning and the management of the educational provision are also measured.
- Trust will be broken and honest feedback will decline if students, staff or parents feel they are not shielded from the potential negative consequences of being honest. In these circumstances people learn quickly to protect themselves and little value is gained from the evaluation exercise.
- Excessive formal monitoring and evaluation exercises take too much time from the main business of school, which is learning.

Tips for evaluating stakeholder suggestions

- Weigh stakeholder suggestions/requests against agreed-upon school values, plans and goals.
- Work through the possible long-term effects/consequences of one stakeholder's suggestions on the entire school and on other stakeholders.
- Weigh the possible reactions of other stakeholders.
- Weigh the possible effects of a proposed change based on student and programme well-being.

Objects of monitoring and evaluation

Students
- learning, achievement and well-being
- engagement
- attendance
- language growth
- communication with L2 speakers (camps, exchanges, projects)
- enrolment and retention rates
- out-of-school L2 use
- satisfaction and intentions
- concerns
- attitudes and behaviour
- autonomy and agency

Staff
- retention rates
- learning and well-being
- training
- stress levels
- sick-leave rates
- mentoring
- sharing of resources
- concerns
- satisfaction and intentions
- attitudes and behaviour
- autonomy and agency

Parents
- concerns
- needs
- quality and extent of engagement
- family learning
- satisfaction and intentions
- attitudes and behaviour
- autonomy and agency

Language
- status of LI, L2, L3
- status of immigrant languages
- use at events, in documents and in signage
- agreement on language use

Learning materials
- quality of L2 materials
- authentic use of authentic materials
- degree of coherence between criteria for learning materials development and the materials being used

Management
- knowledge management
- health and safety
- programme registration and withdrawal procedures
- degree of coherence between plans, actions, budgets, classroom practice, stated values
- decision-making
- levels of improvement
- leadership and management practices

Teaching and learning
- lessons
- teaching practices
- differentiation of learning
- use of information technology
- extra-curricular programme

Documents and events
- plans
- public relations materials
- minutes of meetings
- staff
- inspection reports
- research reports
- school curriculum
- assessment instruments
- school events and meetings

Stakeholder co-operation
- trust (keeping promises, protecting staff/students, respectful behaviour, honesty)
- in-school levels of gossip
- extent and quality of stakeholder engagement
- support for and satisfaction with programme
- conflict resolution and other communications skills
- quality of professional relationships
- attitudes and behaviour
- sources and uptake of information

Personal perspective

Building the foundations

Sandra Lucietto (Istituto Comprensivo Tuenno) is a principal in Italy who is preparing to launch a bilingual programme. She suggests:

Anticipating and navigating external pressure

Some parents pressured me to introduce a bilingual programme immediately. I explained to parents that we were not ready, and needed a full year to prepare. We set up a working group. Now, we all understand better the long-term challenges we are facing. The school governors are pleased and helping to pave the way for programming. We will start programming next year.

Parental desire for programming can in some cases also be combined with pressure from local authorities. Local authorities wanting the best for their community may push too hard for bilingual programmes. Schools need time to prepare. I have seen cases where programmes have been started on weak foundations, and have later proven unsustainable.

Thinking 'system' and 'long-term'

I take a systems-wide view. I have involved non-permanent staff in in-service training for bilingual education. Even if they are not at my school next year, they will be in the system, and the system as a whole will benefit.

Being knowledgeable about bilingual education

I think it is important for the principal to be knowledgeable about the innovation she or he wants to implement, or have a deputy who is.

Recognising effort

We all want to be recognised for our efforts. Recognition can take many forms, including: praise at a whole staff meeting, an article in the local magazine, listening to staff, and professional-development opportunities.

3 Leadership

This chapter focuses on:

- being the instructional/curriculum leader
- using assessment to improve learning and examination results
- building a professional learning community and avoiding pseudo-communities
- developing school unity
- working with local, regional and/or national government authorities
- working with the media.

Being the instructional/curriculum leader

As schools are first and foremost institutions which foster student learning, the principal is logically first and foremost an instructional/curriculum leader. Even if a school has a full-time curriculum co-ordinator other than the principal, a principal sets the tone for a school and ultimately takes responsibility for what is taught and how it is taught. It is the time and space accorded by a principal to key values, and teaching and learning strategies, that sets an example for others and that dictates to a considerable extent the focus of professional dialogue in a school. It is therefore useful if the principal and other school leaders have a common understanding of:

- effective teaching and learning strategies
- the regional, national and/or international curriculum requirements (for schools teaching two or more curricula, how these will be integrated and duplication avoided)
- the social and emotional development needs of students
- how and in which ways a school's extra-curricular activities support and possibly undermine learning
- what is actually taking place in classrooms, during extra-curricular activities and in the school yard and hallways (operational curriculum)

- what are the unwritten student, teacher and parent expectations regarding student learning of both content and language, and what are the rules of social and academic engagement such as who decides what and which types of knowledge are considered worthy or unworthy (hidden curriculum)
- how to help stakeholders maintain a focus on student learning, not just grades
- how to maintain a focus on learning in budgets, planning and public relations documents, professional development initiatives, during school meetings and whilst hiring staff
- how current staff, student, student–student, staff–student, staff–parent and other stakeholder relationships support or undermine learning
- how assessment can support learning for all stakeholders (students, teachers, managers, parents and others) and lead to the improvement of teaching and learning environments and practices.

Developing academic language proficiency

In order to have a reasoned dialogue that leads to a decision to change any given practice in bilingual education, it is helpful to limit the discussion to those key practices that have a significant influence on student learning. For example, it is widely agreed that **students learning through an L2 need to be systematically supported over a period of five to ten years in developing proficiency in the use of academic language.** Major studies in this area focus on students from immigrant backgrounds studying through the language of their host country (see the work of Jim Cummins, Kenji Hakuta and others). Extrapolating from these studies, students in bilingual education also require on-going and systematic support throughout their education in working with academic language and in achieving a high degree of proficiency in its use. Academic language is a key tool used for learning content and for improving the capacity to think about and work with content concepts. Some educators may mistakenly believe that once a student demonstrates that she or he is proficient in using social language the student is also proficient in using academic language.

Teachers have often not been trained in taking on the challenging task of teaching academic language. This language needs to be broken down into its component parts and made visible to students so they can make a conscious effort to learn it and use it. Academic language consists of much more than subject-specific vocabulary and terminology. Academic language has a particular tone; is often evidence-based; uses categories and concepts; has specific functions that may require hypothesising or explaining causes and consequences; is more precise than spoken language; uses conventions such as footnotes; avoids slang; and is often cognitively demanding and context-reduced.[1] For an overview of some of the component parts of the language of Science see pages 46–47.

---

[1]See the work of Jim Cummins on academic and social language.

THE LANGUAGE OF SCIENCE
(for learning Science through English)

Characteristics of scientific language

- special or unique vocabulary
- terminological precision, avoiding pronouns
- concise (avoids repetition), unemotional and factual
- concrete, exact, seeks to allow only one possible interpretation
- evidence-based, uses trustworthy data
- information presented in a logical and sequential manner (in a systematic way)

- uses categories and concepts
- uses tables, diagrams, formulas and figures
- uses footnotes and references
- refers to validity and reliability
- maintains the same tone throughout the text
- sentences often include qualifying clauses
- uses analogies and describes their limitations
- uses both active and passive voice

Avoids certain terms and words

Expressions of absolute certainty (this study proves that / it is certain that / it is a fact that / absolute proof) are avoided, as any one experiment or study rarely leads to a universal truth.

Common functions and activities + related language

arguing, categorising, claiming, classifying, comparing, concluding, contrasting, defining, describing, distinguishing between evidence and interpretation, generalising, hypothesising, identifying, interpreting, labelling, linking, listing, opposing, putting in order (time, weight, size, etc.), predicting, presenting facts, presenting problems and solutions, presuming, recommending, referencing, reporting, separating and explaining causes and consequences, summarising

For example, predicting: I predict that ...; The following result is likely because ...; Based on ...; I foresee ...; The blotter will absorb ...; Scientists believe (think, envisage, calculate) that by the middle of this century ...; By Friday, the plant will probably ...; The properties of this chemical will contribute to ...; It may change in colour, size, weight, etc. ...; It is usually only found in ...

Subject-specific vocabulary

omnivore vs animal that eats all kinds of food; thorax vs area between the head and abdomen; amphibian vs an animal that lives both on land and in water; submarine volcano vs underwater volcano; calorifacient vs fattening; carbohydrate; mineral (inorganic); probability; acidity; saturated

Words that take on an additional or a different meaning in scientific discourse

core (the earth's core vs. an apple core), space (the cosmos vs. on a hard drive), bed (riverbed vs. bed for sleeping), bank (a riverbank vs. an institution), face (face of a cliff vs. a person's face); an assignment (of value vs. a homework assignment); a cell (a cell in the human body vs. for a prisoner)

International terms (Latin + cognates)

per capita, verbatim, bona fide, in vitro, electron, molecule, energy, biology, diffusion, autotroph

Common phrases

At the start of the experiment I ...; Diagram 1 shows (that) ...; This study gives an overview of ...; It is assigned a value of 100 ...; Information in the chart has been gathered from ...; Based on the first example, it is possible to conclude ...; less than, more than, equal amounts; This is likely to be caused by ...; In comparison with a spider, an insect has ...; The butterfly's life-cycle can be divided into ... stages. The first is named the ...; the second ...; Trial and error ...; By substituting the value of X in equation ...; The evidence suggests that ...

Transition words/phrases, connectives, intensives, bridges

For sequencing: first, second, third, initially, at the next stage, finally, eventually, previously. **For concluding:** in summary, in conclusion. **For comparing and contrasting:** however, but, on the other hand, in contrast, in the same way, conversely, on the contrary. **For connecting:** thus, however, furthermore, although, nevertheless. **For intensifying:** particularly, above all, significantly.

Reading and writing strategies

Students can: Analyse the root of words, prefixes and suffixes. Deconstruct compound words. Compare a literary and scientific text. Brainstorm language suitable for writing up experiments. Explain one phenomenon as a lay person, then as a scientist. Put scrambled paragraphs or steps in a logical order. Make predictions based on a heading, a sentence, a paragraph or a picture. Underline words or phrases that build bridges between ideas or paragraphs. Highlight the hypothesis and conclusions. Use diagrams, figures or charts to draw conclusions or write a text. Create subheadings for each paragraph. Identify causes and consequences. Write a summary. Describe an experiment's purpose, required materials, methods and stages, conditions. Write questions a teacher might ask about a text. Role-play. Visualise mental images of scientific processes. Draw out scientific language from three different texts. Develop a glossary of useful scientific terms, and of expressions to be avoided. Review common errors in logic.

Using good pedagogical practices

Bilingual education is not simply a form of language teaching, but of education in general. Because of the additional challenges of learning through an L2, bilingual education calls for the enhanced use of good pedagogical practices in order to give the best possible support to both content and language learning. There is a significant body of research, including research in bilingual education contexts, that demonstrates that the practices being proposed in this guide can help students to learn more language, content and learning skills within a much shorter timeframe, and to achieve much better test results than is the case when these best practices are not applied. The potential gains in time-savings and improved learning are substantial.

This guide offers two instruments that summarise key considerations that have an impact on learning in bilingual education – *A Bilingual Education Continuum* and the *CLIL Essentials*.

A Bilingual Education Continuum

The Bilingual Education Continuum (see pages 50–51) integrates elements of best practice in education in general with those practices favoured by bilingual education. Furthermore, decision-making and teaching practices do not operate strictly on a rational level, but are tied to the affective domain of beliefs and assumptions. Thus, the Continuum depicts a continuous sequence of practices, beliefs and assumptions.

The opposite ends of the Continuum are very distinct and in opposition to one another. These are described in detail in the diagram, but the in-between space and the innumerable number of adjacent elements that sequentially lead to either end of the continuum are left to the imagination. On a practical level, the Continuum is intended as a framework for structuring stakeholder dialogue about individual and group beliefs, assumptions and practices. It is hoped that the act of discussing practices, beliefs and assumptions, whilst plotting them on the Continuum, will support stakeholders in assessing their own and a bilingual programme's current state of development. Stakeholders will be able to discuss where in relation to the Continuum they would like themselves and the programme to be in the future, and how this could be achieved.

This Continuum constitutes a form of high expectations. Successful bilingual education programmes are characterised as having high expectations for students and teachers. It is not expected that all educators will fully meet all these high expectations. They are offered as goals to be worked towards.

Personal perspective

Dramatic arts and language learning

Jane Deluzio is deputy principal in a Canadian high school. She has trained teachers to use Drama in bilingual education. She says:

Drama, which focuses on self-expression (as opposed to theatre arts, where the words of others are presented), is a particularly good subject for teaching through the L2. Drama requires students to find their own words to communicate an important idea during a moment of significance. **Drama provides rich opportunities for meaningful oral and written communication.** Because students role-play a variety of situations in Drama classes, they are required to use a much wider variety of language, including registers of language, than is the case in the average classroom. In addition to language, Drama students learn about tone, levels of formality, speed of delivery and how to listen to others. These are all important life-skills, whether one is speaking the L2 or L1.

L2 Drama can also be used to reinforce work done in other subjects such as History or Science that are being taught through the L2 or even through the L1. For example, by having a student role-play a contagious virus and by talking through the virus' journey with the support of a teacher, the Science curriculum becomes better rooted in the student's memory. The student's understanding of this topic is tested, deepened and probably expanded. **The Drama teacher and the Science teacher** can give a joint mark for this role-play which should further reinforce the serious nature of this learning experience.

CLIL Essentials

The CLIL Essentials framework (see pages 52–53) expands on the practices and some of the beliefs and assumptions listed in the Bilingual Education Continuum.

Using assessment to improve learning and examination results

Assessment is ultimately about **reflection and improving learning**. A school that uses assessment for learning not only reflects on student learning, but works with other stakeholders to reflect on their learning. Assumptions, beliefs, practices, test results, survey findings and documents are analysed. Changes

A BILINGUAL EDUC

FACTORS UNDERMINING MEANINGFUL LEARNING OF CURRICULUM

BELIEFS
- challenging content cannot be taught/learnt through L2
- socially disadvantaged and low-achieving students cannot learn challenging content through L2
- teaching either through L1 or L2 is superior
- teachers just teach their subject(s)
- intuition is always right
- working alone is best

ASSUMPTIONS
- native speakers of L2 can teach through students' L2 without training
- teachers will do what a principal asks
- appearances and assumptions can be taken at face value
- someone who has successfully taught one Grade can teach another
- parents should not interfere in school education

Ineffective Practice

(in classes taught through L2) extensive and non-judicious use of L1 and translation

teacher-talk and activities dominate lessons

initiation-response-feedback pattern and answers for display dominate

characteristics and component parts of academic language are not drawn out

insufficient scaffolding of language or its complete absence

insufficient scaffolding of content or its complete absence

unclear or unstated intended learning outcomes (language, content, learning skills)

no teaching or modelling of learning skills

low expectations re: content and language learning and re: socially disadvantaged students

strong sense of teacher and student disassociation from one another

aggressive, psychologically unsafe climate where many students do not experiment with content and language

high level of teacher attention to control

acquisition of facts as driver of learning

no cross-curricular or cross-cultural links

cognitively unchallenging tasks and low level of student engagement in learning

no authentic materials or communication with L2 speakers

*ZPD = zone of proximal development (see work of Lev Vygotsky)

.TION CONTINUUM

Effective Practice

(in classes taught through L2) limited and judicious use of L1 and translation whilst maintaining learning primarily through L2

student-talk, and engagement in individual and peer co-operative work dominate lessons

dialogic discourse dominates lessons

characteristics and component parts of academic language are drawn out

ample and detailed scaffolding of language while maintaining students in their ZPD*

ample and detailed scaffolding of content while maintaining students in their ZPD

clearly stated intended learning outcomes (language, content, learning skills) and regularly discussing progress against these

teaching and modelling of learning skills ⟨ content / language

high expectations re: content and language learning and re: socially disadvantaged students

strong sense of affiliation between teacher and students

constructive, psychologically safe climate where all students freely experiment with content and language

high level of student decision-making and self-control (autonomy and agency)

critical thinking as driver of learning ⟨ content / language / learning skills

cross-curricular and cross-cultural links

cognitively challenging tasks and high level of student engagement in learning

authentic materials used in authentic ways and guided communication with L2 speakers

FACTORS FOSTERING MEANINGFUL LEARNING OF CURRICULUM

BELIEFS
- challenging content can be taught through L2
- socially disadvantaged and low-achieving students can learn challenging content through L2
- teaching through L2 is valuable if L1 also developed through L1 subject classes
- teachers teach both content and language
- bilingual education is on occasion counterintuitive
- working in co-operation with others is a key value

ASSUMPTIONS
- native speakers of L2 need training in teaching through students' L2
- teachers will make their own decisions based on their own beliefs
- appearances and assumptions need to be questioned/explored
- challenges faced by teachers change from Grade to Grade
- parents are partners in education

CLIL

Quality, ethical CLIL is:

✓ **not** simply a matter of changing the language of instruction

✓ **not** just for high achievers

✓ **not** elitist

✓ **not** a means for suppressing the L1.

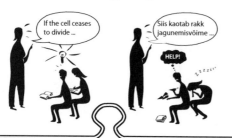

MANAGING THE AFFECTIVE SIDE

CREATING A SECURE LEARNING ENVIRONMENT

✓ students help set rules
✓ no labelling of students
✓ no ridicule or sarcasm

THE INTERDEPENDENCE OF LANGUAGE AND COGNITION

CLIL is a dual-focused teaching and learning approach in which the and an additional language or two are used for promoting both content maste and language acquisition to pre-defined levels.*

FOSTERING CRITICAL THINKING
CONTENT & LANGUAGE

Create

Evaluate

Analyse

Apply

Understand

Remember
(= knowledge in Bloom's taxonomy)

(Anderson, Krathwohl *et al.*, 2000)

TAKING TIME FOR MAKING LEARNING MEANINGFUL

✓ not just concentrating on understanding
✓ fostering relational links (e.g. drawing out and linking key concep
✓ connecting with students' interests

FOSTERING LEARNER AUTONOMY

✓ giving students choices to make
✓ teaching learning skills
✓ negotiating decisions about the learning process with students

CO-OPERATIVE LEARNING

✓ positive interdependence
✓ face-to-face promotive interaction
✓ individual and group accountability
✓ interpersonal and small group skills
✓ group processing

(Johnson and Johnson, 2001)

Designed: www.tm.ee

* This definition builds on a definition by Maljers *et al.* (2007), and has benefited from personal communication with Genesee (2010) and Frigols Martin (

© Mehisto and Lucietto (2011)

:SSENTIALS

MAKING INTENDED LEARNING EXPLICIT & VISIBLE

I WANT TO KNOW HOW PLANES FLY.

W TO FIND RMATION HE SCHOOL ARY.

... THE PAST TENSE.

STUDENTS SEE & DISCUSS CONTENT, LANGUAGE & LEARNING SKILLS OUTCOMES

Content
1. You can name in writing the fifteen major tectonic plates.

2. You can explain how tectonic plates affect one another.

Language
3. You can use analogies in scientific descriptions, including explaining their limitations.

Learning skills
4. You will be able to summarise other students' ideas.

tectonic plates affect one another
make up the earth's crust
form major tectonic plates
are in constant movement
pass each other
collide into each other
move under (on top of) each other
melt into molten rock
become magma
release gases
cause volcanic eruptions

to move as slowly as fingernails grow
Shield volcanoes resemble a Roman soldier's shield lying on the ground.

'MJ predicts that the next level-seven eruption will occur in Italy in ..., because on average there is a level-seven eruption every ... years.'

HIGH EXPECTATIONS + HIGH LEVELS OF ENGAGEMENT FOR ALL

MAKING ACADEMIC LANGUAGE VISIBLE
e.g., discourse patterns, connectors, academic registers (e.g., tone, fact-based, unemotional, avoidance of 1st person), phrases for analysis and discussion, …

REFLECTING ON LEARNING

Every day discussing with students:
✓ progress in meeting learning outcomes
✓ the learning process
✓ what to change / how to move forward.

SCAFFOLDING CONTENT

e.g., using advance and other graphic organisers; highlighting key facts; using plenty of subheadings; using analogies; building on students' existing skills, knowledge and understandings; reducing the number of problems or facts presented at one time; teaching learning skills; …

REFLECTING ON TEACHING

✓ leading by example / showing that you too are a learner
✓ assessing and discussing your own work

SCAFFOLDING LANGUAGE

e.g., using short sentences and paragraphs, repeating nouns instead of using pronouns, underlining key phrases, brainstorming topic-related language, students writing own definitions, organising vocabulary in categories, pre-using vocabulary and discourse patterns …

CONNECTING WITH CLIL LANGUAGE SPEAKERS AND THEIR CULTURE(S)

e.g., email projects, student exchanges, Internet forums, partner schools, e-pals, analysing how two cultures view one historical or cultural event, …

ASYMMETRY IN CLASSROOM TALK IN FAVOUR OF STUDENTS

✓ more 'exploratory talk', as opposed to 'presentational talk' (Barnes, 1997)
✓ students speak, read and write more than the teacher

in understandings take place and stakeholders including principals, teachers, parents and students make changes in their practices in order to facilitate student learning. Not all student assessments take the form of a mark/grade, but seek rather to improve the learning environment and support students in better managing their own learning.

Examinations and good pedagogical practices

When a school emphasises final examination results over good pedagogical practices, the quality of relationships and learning, it is likely to do a disservice to its students, teachers, parents and community. In situations where examination results are overemphasised, the focus of learning may become restricted. Principals and teachers tend to become less creative. Teaching to the exam may become the norm. Even when student examination results improve, **students' motivation to learn may decline.** In contrast, in schools where aspects of good pedagogy such as fostering critical thinking and learner autonomy are stressed, and where students, teachers and principals feel a strong sense of affiliation with one another, **examination results tend to improve** without the accompanying negative consequences typical of high-stakes situations. However, as high-stakes examinations are a reality in many parts of the world, it is important also to teach students how to prepare for and take these tests. (See www.cie.org.uk for tips on preparing for and taking examinations.)

Assessment for learning

In addition to standard assessment requirements, in bilingual education the following are also assessed by schools.

- **Achievement of content and language goals.** If content and language goals are not assessed and discussed in all classes, students are less likely to be able to manage their own learning of both. Although people do not require language to think, it plays an important role in developing the capacity to think. Thus, content teachers need to help students to improve their language skills, because improved language skills can contribute to improved thinking skills and content learning.

- **Comprehension and ability to use L2 to work with content versus degrees of control over language use.** It is important to be able to separate content from language. For example, this could involve according 95–100% of marks in a content subject test for content as opposed to language. Some schools provide 5% in extra points for accurate and sophisticated use of language, or simply provide anecdotal feedback on progress in using academic language.

- **Ongoing language growth.** There is a tendency for students to reach a plateau in their language development, after which language learning may slow down. Once students can communicate with ease with content teachers through the L2, they may not seek to improve their L2 language skills unless content teachers set higher language learning expectations for them.

- **Achievement of learning-skills goals.** This includes assessing the extent to which the student is an autonomous learner of content, language and learning skills. There is a strong link between the extent to which students can draw on learning skills for the learning of content, language and learning in general, and student achievement.[2] Research has demonstrated that when faced with difficult tasks, learning skills are a stronger indicator of high levels of student achievement than intelligence as measured by IQ tests.

- **Use of language for various purposes.** These include academic, social and business registers.

- **All four language skills.** Listening, speaking, reading and writing are processed in different places in the brain. Using all four language skills creates additional neuronal links, enriches a person's understanding of a given topic, and helps to make learning more meaningful. Moreover, listening, speaking, reading and writing are all central to communication within and across language groups.

- **Ability to work with authentic materials.** Ideally, written and oral texts from various media, articles or other genuine materials created by L2 speakers are used in teaching and learning and, therefore, also used in assessment.

- **Ability to communicate with native and non-native speakers of the L2.**

- **Extent to which students experiment with language and content.**

- Cognition or thinking is created through social interaction. Without active participation, learning opportunities are restricted. Thus, learning **environments are assessed to determine how they help students to feel safe,** to manage their emotions, and to engage actively in learning.

Assessing language use in content classes

A major challenge in bilingual education is to distinguish between **content and language errors** on school content tests. Although content teachers assess above all content, they and their students need to assess students' use of language. If language learning is not assessed in content classes (for a grade or not), it tends to slow down or stop.

However, it is important that students are not simply given a small percentage of their content grade for (or other feedback on) the quality of

[2]See the work of Anna U. Chamot, and Marcel V. J. Veenman, Frans J. Prins and Jan J. Elshout.

language in general. The language grade or other **feedback should be tied to specific planned language learning goals/outcomes** – for example, the correct use of comparative clauses or certain phrases and structures that are commonly used in a discipline. This will allow students to make a conscious effort to learn these aspects of language. (See also page 40–41 for language proficiency standards that can be used to assess student learning.) In addition, content teachers can at each grade or level agree on a **common language goal for a week** that all teachers emphasise. This is a particularly useful strategy for rooting out fossilised errors. The chosen language goal can be the object of assessment.

Portfolios

Portfolios are a particularly suitable tool for bilingual education. They are usually **multimodal** in nature (e.g. videos, sound files, electronic or hard-copy pictures and texts). Thus, material in the portfolio can take many forms and all four language skills are required to build the portfolio and for students to explain their choices and plans.

Portfolios consist of a student's most valued work collected over a period of time. This work is related to **intended learning outcomes**. When reviewing their portfolio, students are asked to reflect on both content and language learning, and their development of learning skills. Based on an analysis of their work, students are invited to set new realistic learning goals/outcomes and to develop a plan for achieving these.

Portfolios are often avoided because teachers see them as time-consuming. However, portfolios can be **time-saving devices**. For example, they can be incorporated into an existing routine of parent–teacher meetings and become their central focus. These meetings can be changed into student–parent–teacher meetings. Using portfolios tends to support students in taking greater **responsibility for their own learning**, hence saving teachers time in the long run.

Assessment tips

- Students are more likely to seriously weigh and take into account feedback about a specific piece of work before handing it in for marking. They are less likely to retain and apply feedback regarding a completed assignment.
- If students regularly graph their marks, they are more aware of them, and more likely to take concrete measures to improve learning.

Personal perspective

Meeting educational objectives in Dhaka, Bangladesh

Syeda Madiha Murshed (Managing Director, Scholastica) is responsible for the academic programme for a school in Dhaka, Bangladesh. She suggests:

Identifying objectives

Our school aims to prepare its students not only to be global citizens, but also to have strong roots in their local language, culture and heritage. Therefore, a well-designed curriculum has to meet both these objectives.

Designing a curriculum to meet objectives

At our school, there is an early and continued emphasis on the L2 medium of instruction (English), as the students need extra time and effort to develop their L2 skills to be able to succeed in international examinations, which are held at the end of their secondary schooling. At the same time, students develop their L1 (Bangla) from an early age, not only through language and literature as core subjects, but also through a subject called Bangladesh Studies, which develops historical and geographical subject-knowledge and skills.

Being aware of L1 status and input

Our social context allows us to place an emphasis on the L2 at school because the L1 is the majority language of the national community and is therefore naturally reinforced at home and in the wider community. However, a different L1:L2 educational balance may be required in other contexts where the L1 may be at risk.

Enabling students to operate nationally or internationally

Our students can be called 'bilingual' because they are able to communicate more or less equally in both languages at age-appropriate levels. Although many of our students go abroad for higher education, many also choose to enrol in a local university or to work in a local company. Their bilingual upbringing and education helps them not only to be successful but also in many cases to excel. Our students would probably need to study specialised terminology in certain subjects if they were to attend a local university (where the L1 is the medium of education) or if they were to take a job in a specialised industry. However, most of our graduates go on to academic and professional careers where the level of proficiency they have acquired in the L1 is adequate.

Notes of caution

- Caution is called for in assessing students who have an L1 that differs from the school's L1 and L2 and who have not yet developed academic language proficiency in the school's languages of instruction. If these students are not occasionally tested in their L1, or using other appropriate measures designed for testing students with limited language proficiency in the school's L1, they may be inaccurately assessed. In the worst-case scenario, these students may be designated as having a non-language related special need, and be placed in an impoverished learning environment that does not fully challenge them in learning both content and language.
- Perhaps more surprisingly, caution is also called for when a student comes to school fluent in the school's two languages of instruction. If teachers or those assessing these students at the start of programming or in the early years view them from a monolingual perspective, assessing them only through the school's L1, the conclusions drawn from the assessment will be incomplete and probably inaccurate.

Building a professional learning community and avoiding pseudo-communities

Professional learning communities

There is considerable evidence that student learning improves when a school and its community of stakeholders co-operate and are themselves focused on their own and student learning.

A professional learning community is an inclusive group of people, motivated by a shared learning vision, who support and work with each other, finding ways, inside and outside their immediate community, to enquire on their practice and together learn new and better approaches that will enhance all pupils' learning.[3]

Bolam *et al.*, who undertook an extensive literature review, administered and analysed questionnaires from 393 schools and undertook 16 case studies, concluded that professional learning communities tend to:

- have shared values and visions
- assume collective responsibility for student learning

[3]Stoll *et al.* (2006). *Professional Learning Booklet 1.*

- foster reflective professional inquiry
- facilitate collaboration, which includes open and frank debate
- promote group, as well as individual, learning.[4]

Professional learning communities **emphasise learning,** and thereby **de-emphasise positional power** that emanates from the legal, formal authority of a leader's position. This does not point to a decline in the role assumed by formal leaders, but instead indicates a shift in their practice 'to build leadership capacities in others, and to monitor the leadership work of those others'.[5] The definition of professional learning communities implies that the complexities of education are such that one leader alone could not retain all the knowledge or have the capacity needed to manage programming. Learning is at the centre of a professional learning community, and this **gives knowledge** about practices that need to change, and knowledge about how to do so **a considerable measure of power.** It gives shared knowledge a form of positional power and influence, and thereby, a key role in leadership. As professional learning communities call on schools and their stakeholders to identify and assess their own needs, it places a significant part of the responsibility for improving education on its members.

Although professional learning communities need to use planning and learning tools, as well as follow procedures, these communities are built through interaction. Relationships drive interaction; hence it is the **quality of relationships** that make or break a school.

Pseudo-communities

It is possible for a school to leave the impression that all is well and that staff, students and other stakeholders are working to build a professional learning community when this is not the case. Instead a pseudo-community may have developed and be gaining strength.[6]

In a pseudo-community, common values are not shared. A pseudo-community **avoids frank and open talk,** and suppresses conflict and joint decision-making. A pseudo-community expects its members to give the appearance of congenial face-to-face relations and never to intrude on issues of personal space whilst giving the impression that everything is fine.

[4]Bolam *et al.* (2005). *Creating and Sustaining Effective Professional Learning Communities.* Bristol: University of Bristol.
[5]Leithwood *et al.* (2007). Distributing Leadership to Make Schools Smarter. *Leadership and Policy in Schools* 6(1) 37–67.
[6]See the work of Pamela Grossman, Sam Wineburg and Steven Woolworth.

Pseudo-communities tightly regulate the expression of conflict and dissent, relegating disagreements away from full community discussions to one-on-one interactions. Conversations remain at a very general level, so people can accord their own meaning to these generalities. People can hold onto their current understandings without having them challenged. In pseudo-communities teachers do not readily open their classrooms for others to view their lessons.

In such environments, it is **difficult** or impossible **to subject assumptions, terms, plans or practices to a rigorous process of critical thought** and analysis, or to build a common vision and goals. If left unchallenged, a pseudo-community, in comparison to a professional learning community, would, owing to its inauthentic nature, constitute for its members an impoverished learning environment.

Furthermore, **suppressed conflict** is far from inert. It often **surfaces in covert ways.** In pseudo-communities people are more likely to resist change and to withdraw mentally or physically. By working to deconstruct pseudo-communities and to build a professional learning community, a school can reduce the number of people working at cross-purposes and help increase co-ordinated actions to achieve jointly planned outcomes. However, this will require skill in conflict resolution. Many people and organisations are conflict-adverse, and lack the skill in managing conflict in a constructive manner.[7] One suggested strategy is giving less voice to those people who are not prepared to act as learners and who have difficulty being constructive, and giving greater voice to those whose inquiry is the most thorough and aligned with the institution's agreed goals and vision. This may help build constructive synergy.

 Personal perspective

Managing educational innovation in a Dutch school
Andre Piketh (Stedelijk College, Eindhoven, the Netherlands) is a Senior Teacher responsible for Educational Research and Development. He suggests:

Change
As with any educational change, the implementation of a bilingual programme may meet resistance or a healthy dose of scepticism. The advantage for the Netherlands is that the innovation started at ground level.

[7]See the work of Kerry Patterson, Joseph Grenny, Ron McMillan, Al Switzler, who suggest ways of managing crucial confrontations.

Funding

Extra funding is needed for things such as curriculum development, teacher training and international exchange programmes. Any extra charge to parents can raise questions about the affordability and elitist nature of bilingual education. In our school, a procedure exists to support students who are economically disadvantaged.

Access

Originally only students destined for university could enrol in the bilingual programme. Some schools have since broadened their intake procedures to include students in vocational education.

Whole school

It is important to guard against the perception that all innovative educational initiatives take place within the bilingual programme or that all the dynamic teachers are concentrated in that programme. If you want to maintain a whole-school identity, make sure the bilingual programme is introduced as a whole-school development project. This can be done by stressing the continued importance of L1 and by recognising and building on the skills that students bring from the L1 programme to the bilingual one.

Methodology

Subject teachers teaching through the L2 need to be aware of students' L2 limitations, yet at the same time are expected to teach the same amount of subject-content as in the average L1 classroom. To solve this paradox, content and language integrated learning (CLIL) is our preferred didactic approach. Applying best practice in CLIL is essential to building a quality bilingual programme.

Networks

Creating networks is also central to delivering quality programming. In the Netherlands we have a bilingual school network, a bilingual standard, and a government-financed agency called the European Platform (Europees Platform) that supports programming and does quality control. The European Platform works with international organisations. However, contexts differ from country to country and indeed within countries. Still, there is no need to reinvent the wheel, in terms of bilingual education. It is more a matter of finding the right set of wheels.

Developing school unity

A sense of belonging is a fundamental need. By making a conscious effort to include all staff in a whole-school ethos, it is less likely that groups will emerge that work at cross-purposes. Ideally, those teaching through the L1, those teaching through the L2, experienced and inexperienced teachers, L1 and L2 language teachers, administrators and support staff all operate as one team. Unity results from giving people a voice, negotiating a common vision, and co-operative planning, inquiry and delivery, whilst working towards common goals. In order to build school unity, the following considerations have been reported by principals and/or researchers in bilingual education.

Budget

Budgetary resources

Budgetary resources are used in a fair and equitable manner between the bilingual and regular programme. Even if the school is teaching primarily through the L2, L1 teaching and learning need to be equitably resourced.

Developing the budget

The school team is drawn into developing the budget. During the programme start-up phase, extra resources are required for purchasing learning materials and for staff professional development. Depending on the L2 involved, the learning materials may be more expensive as they need to be tailored for those learning through the L2, and that market may be a small one. Bilingual programme managers will also have to demonstrate their willingness to support other school initiatives.

School governing body

Opportunities for increased understanding

The governing body is provided with rich and varied opportunities to learn about bilingual education and/or the school's bilingual programme so that its members can make informed decisions and act as programme advocates. This is the case whether the impetus for establishing or expanding a bilingual programme comes from the school's governing body or from other school stakeholders.

Representation

Bilingual and regular programme parents are fairly represented on the governing body so that the interests of both programmes are respected.

Responsibilities

The governing body reviews and approves plans, evaluates progress in achieving targets and offers advice. It assumes some responsibilities associated with the implementation of the school's strategic plan, including the development of the bilingual programme.

Language status

- School assemblies use both the L1 and L2 for presentations. Care is taken not to restrict the use of one language for folklore and history, and another for discussing contemporary and possibly higher-status topics such as information technologies, science and economics.
- All languages used for instruction deserve equal consideration during timetabling. For example, classes taught through the L2 may be taught alternately during the mornings one week, and in the afternoons during the next week.
- Both the L1 and the L2 are used for the teaching of high-status subjects.
- Staff have discussed and agreed on language usage in hallways (e.g. L2 usage in hallways can contribute to its meaningful use in new contexts). Unless the L2 is used outside the classroom, it will not have equal status.
- Signs are in both the L1 and L2. Different signs use the languages in a different order. Size and typeface of text reflects equal respect for both languages.
- Extra-curricular activities take place in both the L1 and the L2.
- If the school offers meals, menus are bilingual.
- Staff members agree on strategies for ensuring that the various accents and regional variations of language being used are shown equal respect. For example, some teachers may have a preference for a certain type of L1 or L2, and may require support in accepting a wider variety of language variations.
- Opportunities are sought to raise the visibility of other languages taught in the school and of immigrant languages.
- A multicultural project, exhibition or evening can be organised to showcase the contribution of diverse cultures and language groups to literature, music, science, sport, and so on.
- Performers and guest speakers invited to the school include both those who use the L1 and those who use the L2.

Leading by example

- The principal uses both languages. If he or she does not speak the L2, it is advisable to begin to learn it.
- The principal gives equal attention to those teaching through both languages. This can involve taking guests to see both lessons taught through

the L2 and those taught through the L1. Many school visitors only wish to visit lessons taught through the L2. Attention given by visitors only to bilingual-programme students can leave regular-programme students and staff feeling that they are not fully valued. Even in schools teaching primarily through the L2, teachers teaching through the L1 need to be involved in meeting visitors, otherwise the status of the L1 will be seen to decline.

Staffing

- When hiring teachers to teach through the L1, it is recommended that their attitude regarding the L2 and bilingual education be assessed. It can be helpful if they are bilingual.
- A school's bilingual ethos can be strengthened if support staff such as secretaries, cafeteria workers and cleaners speak both languages.
- The school librarian needs to be bilingual or be prepared to learn the language.

Building harmony

- A conscious effort is made to avoid power imbalances. For example, often the first people to teach through the L2 receive more training than those who join a programme later on. By having well-trained staff who become mentors for other staff, and by consciously valuing the sharing of knowledge, a school can decrease opportunity and knowledge hoarding.
- Visitors are taken to see the lessons of inexperienced as well as experienced teachers. This counters a tendency found in some research studies where experienced teachers have their lessons observed more often than inexperienced teachers. In such circumstances the experienced teachers benefit from increased professional dialogue about their teaching, an opportunity also needed by inexperienced teachers.
- Teachers teaching through the L1 need to be as well trained as those teaching through the L2, or they may be seen as old-fashioned by students and other staff members. Moreover, students may clash with these teachers if their approach to teaching and learning differs greatly from those teaching through the L2.
- Sometimes tensions can emerge between content and language teachers. L2 language teachers may feel marginalised by L2 content teachers or vice versa as each group defends its territory without realising that content and language are both central to the learning process. Language teachers may also feel content teachers' L2 skills are not strong enough for teaching their subject through the L2. Content teachers may not understand their own language-related needs or know how to support the learning of academic language.

- Both content and language teachers may need guidance in how to work together. This may involve having teachers from another school share how they organise co-operation between content and language teachers. In addition, if language teachers take on extra duties in supporting content teachers this may need to be recognised in some meaningful way by school management. Equally importantly, as content teachers take on the role of systematically supporting language learning this needs to be acknowledged and managed.

- Teachers teaching through the L1 and the L2 need structured opportunities to share teaching experiences, learning materials and strategies. In addition, time is needed to plan for cross-curricular integration.

- All teachers may require support in ensuring that all students in the bilingual (and regular programme) are valued, and given the support needed to meet high expectations. Additional professional development in offering students differentiated learning opportunities may be needed.

- There should be an inclusive rewards and recognition policy that fosters recognising all students and staff.

Stakeholder motivations

Any individual stakeholder or group of stakeholders may have different motivations for supporting the programme, and these are always likely to be changing on some level. Regularly drawing out each person's or group's understandings, analysing what is possible, and agreeing on common goals and ways of achieving them should help to increase unity.

Working with local, regional and/or national government authorities

The role of authorities

The success of a bilingual programme is often closely tied to the level of support it receives from the local, regional and/or national government authorities, who can assume various roles as outlined below.

Foundations

- establish a policy and regulatory framework for bilingual education
- co-ordinate and promote bilingual programmes, which includes assigning this responsibility to an official or a group of officials
- commit publicly to the delivery of bilingual programming throughout primary, secondary and vocational school so as to build confidence in parents and students

- build continuity in bilingual education across primary, secondary and vocational schools
- facilitate, finance or organise professional development for bilingual education inspectors, principals and teachers
- assess teachers' linguistic skills in cases where principals are not highly proficient in the L2

Leadership

- exercise leadership in bilingual programme development and expansion
- set and support the meeting of high expectations in bilingual education (student learning, professional conduct, stakeholder relations)
- identify research needs and finance research initiatives (e.g. regarding bilingual programme management, student achievement and stakeholder satisfaction and concerns)
- lobby (in the case of local or regional authorities) national organisations for additional support
- recognise and reward individual and group achievement (students, parents, educators and other stakeholders)
- provide management guidelines to principals of bilingual schools
- create L2 public-speaking forums such as debating competitions and Science Olympics

Communications

- develop information materials on bilingual education
- ensure bilingual education is visible in a broad range of public relations instruments such as an authority's annual reports, newsletters, videos and website

Co-operation

- facilitate local, regional or national networking opportunities for stakeholder groups such as teachers and principals, and across stakeholder groups (e.g. schools, teacher-training institutions, research institutes, parent groups, inspectors and learning materials developers)
- facilitate opportunities for inter-regional/international networking with practitioners and experts in the field, including by identifying and backing the launch of inter-regional and international projects supporting bilingual education
- lobby universities to provide opportunities for secondary school graduates to continue their studies (at the tertiary level) partially through the school system's L2

Resources

- source and purchase exemplary L2 materials for student learning and educator professional development
- develop a database of recommended L2 learning materials (e.g. readers, textbooks, websites and software).

Working with authorities

Although the role of local, regional and national authorities is to help build conditions that support schools, authorities need considerable input from these schools in order to understand how best to do this. In other words, by working closely with authorities schools can help keep them informed, make proposals and generally help build a context that is favourable to bilingual education.

Inter-school co-operation

Options include:

- creating an advisory committee of principals, or a committee of principals, parents, teachers, teacher trainers that: a) identifies successful measures introduced by the authorities that support bilingual programming; b) identifies bilingual programme successes and lessons learned; c) makes recommendations to authorities for change
- working with other schools to provide feedback on draft policies
- including local authorities in discussions when building ties with employers, chambers of commerce, museums, libraries and other stakeholders
- encouraging authorities to ask museums and libraries that fall under their jurisdiction to support L2 learning (e.g. libraries can be encouraged to purchase L2 books, films and music, as well as to do story-time in the L2)
- encouraging authorities to make agreements with other authorities in order to foster student exchanges and other forms of co-operation
- encouraging authorities to maintain a database of all bilingual schools so as to facilitate inter-school co-operation and so families that move to a new area can rapidly find the nearest bilingual school
- contributing to the development of a bilingual education policy through participation in committees and work groups and through lobbying
- participating in special-needs committees or workshops to help ensure that bilingual education needs are factored into planned special education initiatives
- encouraging officials to attend key conferences about bilingual education
- making a joint presentation at a conference with an official.

Worldwide school partnership programmes

Schools can join worldwide school partnership programmes. This can be done with a view to fostering regional and international co-operation and to making the local authority visible. These worldwide programmes provide opportunities for students to work on joint projects using their L2 and content subject knowledge. Teachers can share video clips of lessons, lesson plans and learning materials. Principals can share leadership concerns and strategies. For example: British Council Connecting Classrooms (www. britishcouncil.org/learning-connecting-classrooms.htm); BBC World Class www.bbc.co.uk/ worldclass/); Association for Science Education's Science Across the World (www.ase.org.uk/resources/science-across-the-world/); The CLIL Cascade Network (www.ccn-clil.eu/).

In school

Schools can work with authorities by:

- inviting them to attend and speak at school events such as conferences, home–school meetings and graduation ceremonies (e.g. having an official open a school conference)
- recognising in school documents, at school events or when speaking at regional or national events the contributions made by authorities
- creating value for the authorities by actively participating in initiatives which they undertake
- offering the school as a showcase where authorities are welcome to bring guests
- keeping authorities informed by sharing annual reports, public relations documents and putting authorities on the school's mailing list (also over-communication is not advised).

Working with the media

Bilingual schools often come under greater media scrutiny than regular monolingual schools. This raises the need for principals of bilingual schools to be adept at working with the media. Considerable support can be built for bilingual education through a public relations and media (PR) strategy.

However, a school must first have a reputation for caring about two-way communication. This would involve promptly returning phone calls, answering emails and making visitors feel welcome, as well as listening to and taking into account parental concerns. Without having these fundamental practices and values in place, it is difficult to trust a school's PR messages.

In order to develop a coherent set of PR messages, it is first necessary to have an agreement on core values and plans. Successes and challenges need to be identified. In particular, it is useful to identify short-term wins or successes such as a school conference or a student exchange visit/programme. These short-term wins will help others see that academic success and the learning of a language are part of a lengthy process consisting of many elements and stages.

A PR strategy is as much about internal as it is about external communication and co-operation. The strategy would include listening to and trying to address the concerns of stakeholders. It is tied to a school's rewards and recognition policy. It involves agreeing on key messages that the school wants to communicate. Moreover, by making a school's intentions/plans and messages public, a school becomes more accountable. People are more likely to do something when they have publicly stated their plans. The following PR strategies do not represent a full set of expectations that a bilingual school must meet. Instead, it is hoped that the following PR strategies, which have been used by bilingual schools, can serve as a resource in planning a school's own strategy.

PR strategies

Stakeholder recognition

A conscious effort is made to recognise the contributions of all stakeholders. For example, the support of the local authority or of a parent council is recognised at public events and in school documents. This also contributes to the motivation of school stakeholders. It increases the possibility that these individuals will support your school and the bilingual programme.

High-status individuals

Well-known academics, business people, sports personalities or other high-status individuals such as diplomats can befriend a school. By doing so, they lend their status to the school. More specifically, these individuals can be quoted in a school brochure and they can speak at a school assembly or conference about the importance of bilingualism.

Brochures and folders

A one-page, fold-out leaflet can provide considerable information about the bilingual programme such as: goals, key facts from research that address parental concerns, short quotations from two high-status individuals about bilingualism, some of the benefits of bilingual education, and where to find more information.

Newsletters or blogs

A hardcopy or electronic newsletter can showcase students and teachers. It can be limited to two pages per month. Often parent volunteers can support a school in producing blogs and/or newsletters, as some parents may be experts in communication or design. In addition to improving the quality of a product, parental involvement can also increase the likelihood that the newsletter or blog addresses parental concerns. A newsletter can be sent home with the students or where possible by email. They can also be sent to local officials and the media. Newsletters can be made available on a school's home page on the internet.

Issues management

Issues that could influence the bilingual programme and its stakeholders are identified. Strategies are created to respond to these issues.

Media monitoring

Relevant media (local, regional, national) are monitored to analyse how bilingual education is perceived and to identify issues that could influence the school. Some teachers and parents can assume part of this monitoring responsibility.

Media relations

Informal and formal contacts are fostered with journalists or news agencies. Most major newspapers have an education desk. A school can offer the media human-interest stories, for example about school events, student and staff achievements, profiles of retiring school staff, profiles of new staff, and stories about successful graduates. A school can invite a journalist to a school event, and provide this person with the school's annual report, brochures and interesting photographs. These will facilitate the journalist's work.

Notes of caution

Identify a journalist who is known for being constructive.

Journalists often keep silent for a long time after someone answers a question, hoping that the person will keep speaking. When you have finished saying what you have to say, do not feel you have to fill the silence. Smile and wait for the next question.

Never say anything in confidence (off the record) that you would not want printed. If you do not know the answer, do not speculate.

Offer to read the draft of the article the journalist writes before it is published, to point out misquotations or inaccuracies. This is not, however, something to insist on, but is rather an option to be offered.

In radio or television interviews, sometimes only one sentence from an interview is used. Any sentence you say has to be able to stand on its own.

Always take the time to thank the journalist for his/her time and interest.

If a report is inaccurate and you think this could have serious implications for the school, quickly contact the journalist or the media outlet and ask for an opportunity for a rebuttal.

Media partnership

A school can work with a media partner in the long term to foster an understanding of bilingual education issues.

Conferences

A school can organise a conference for parents, its own teachers, teachers from nearby schools and/or students.

Open house

Once or twice a year a school can open its doors to the public. Groups of visitors are given opportunities to visit certain classes, see student exhibitions, speak with staff and students, and attend an assembly. This is an opportunity for sharing key messages. In addition to using a school day for the open house, a non-work day morning can be used to invite the community to visit the school and to meet staff and students. This will facilitate the participation of working people.

Connecting with other PR strategies

A local government or education authority may have its own PR strategy. It may be possible to link with events included in that PR strategy. The local government or education authority may have its own PR officer who may be happy to publicise your school's good-news stories.

Professional development

It is a good idea for schools to provide staff and parents, who are involved with PR initiatives, relevant professional development opportunities.

Problems and solutions

School-related problems that have made it into the public domain need to be dealt with honestly. It is important to know and stick to the facts, to avoid blame, to explain that problems are a normal part of school life, and to focus on solutions.

4 Students

This chapter focuses on:

- supporting and retaining students
- addressing potential gender issues.

Supporting and retaining students

Ultimately, this entire guide is about creating environments that support students in learning. The following are some additional strategies used by bilingual schools to support and retain students.

School climate and ethos

Creating a psychologically safe learning environment

Learning through an L2 (see pages 45, 50–53) poses an extra challenge to students. All students in the classroom need to feel free to experiment with the additional language and to make use of their right to participate in activities and communication without being afraid of making mistakes.

Developing a 'can-do' 'growth mind-set' in students and staff[1]

High expectations and a belief that all students can learn through the L2 are a key feature of successful bilingual education. To achieve this, staff must have high expectations for themselves both individually and collectively.

Avoiding the 'blame game' and the labelling of students

Schools that avoid labelling students as weak or bright and their parents as educated or uneducated, and instead concentrate on richly scaffolding all

[1]See the work of Carol Dweck on 'fixed mind-sets' versus 'growth mind-sets'.

students' learning so high expectations can be met, tend to have significantly better examinations results.

Avoiding the labelling of teachers

This is central to maintaining the motivation and high expectations of all teachers.

Enshrining the support of others as a school value

During lessons, group and pair work should be regularly analysed and assessed with this value in mind. Staff and students can be recognised and rewarded for making a particular effort in supporting others.

Fostering a climate of inclusion

Staff may need support in ensuring that all students and cultures present in the school are valued. For example, by allowing immigrant students to write part of a report in their L1 or encouraging their parents to foster L1 literacy in the home, the school demonstrates that it values immigrant languages and cultures.

Mechanisms

Instituting a buddy system

Students can be paired to help each other. As part of the assessment process, buddies can analyse the effectiveness of the processes and strategies they are using to learn.

Getting senior students to help younger students

This can be organised on an individual basis after or during class, or an entire class of senior students can help an entire class of junior students. Students helping others are recognised for their work (e.g. by a reception in the principal's office, letters of commendation, excursions).

Asking parent volunteers to help students

This technique is often used with younger students.

Capturing explanations in videos

Ten- to fifteen-minute videos in which a teacher explains a key concept can be uploaded to a school intranet site or home page, or to a free video-sharing website. Not only can students then return to these as many times as they wish, but teachers using this technique are likely to invest more time and thought in their explanations; they may also create graphic organisers to explain their point or to draw out new language (see www.khanacademy.org/).

Instituting a school-wide, multi-year, learning-skills development programme

Teaching learning skills helps learners to help themselves. Strategies can be taught to improve reading, writing and the management of one's emotions. To improve reading comprehension, students can be first taught to survey a text looking at diagrams, subheadings and conclusions, and scanning for a few unfamiliar words to be looked up in a dictionary. Numerous strategies can also be taught to unlock the meaning of unfamiliar words, such as deconstructing compound words or using context to guess at meaning. To improve their own writing, students can learn to proofread a text several times for specific purposes such as checking for spelling and the logical sequencing and clarity of ideas.

Contact and communication with peers and adults who speak the L2

This helps to put learning to practical use and motivate students. Meeting peers can be highly motivating and provide opportunities to learn a different and vibrant register of speech, and to develop cultural insights. Meetings with adults (e.g. employers, community leaders, representatives of various professions, the elderly, young entrepreneurs, former students) provide additional registers of speech. They also help students to set long-term goals, develop learning skills, see evidence of the value of the L2, and gain important cultural and other insights into the adult world in which they will soon be playing their part.

Having teachers on call

A teacher or two can be on call several times a week at a specific time to help students. These teachers can be available in a classroom, on the phone, through email, using free voice-over-internet providers, or by other electronic means.

Supporting homework clubs and group study

Supporting the development of homework clubs and teaching students how to manage group study sessions can help them to become more effective and autonomous learners.

Management strategies

Offering an extended day programme

This will allow students a greater opportunity to use the L2 and for teachers to support learning. Extended time is meant to be used differently from regular class time. As well as being used for co-curricular activities (e.g. such as a Science club which does investigations into or experiments in the community) extended time can be used for doing homework, which can take considerable pressure off parents and students.

Front-loading a programme with the best-trained teachers

The teachers who teach students at the start of the programme play a central role in their development, and will continue to have an influence on their learning and achievement for years to come. In particular, **low-achieving students are thought to be the first to benefit and to benefit the most from**

effective teaching. High achievers also benefit. However, as high achievers bring greater resources to the learning process and already have high grades, their improvement, as measured by grades, is less.

Care should be taken to ensure that the most vulnerable students have the best-trained teachers. Situations where a low-achieving student is assigned for two terms or years in a row to a teacher who has not been prepared for bilingual education need to be avoided.

Identifying early the challenges teachers are facing

Early identification of the almost inevitable challenges teachers face is central to the building of quality learning environments. Because of the additional demands of bilingual education, teachers require an additional measure of support to identify and solve the challenges they face, so that they can better support students. This can include mentoring, regular opportunities for a professional exchange of ideas about teaching/learning with the principal or deputy principal and targeted in-service training.

Testing early for phonological awareness

In cases where students are studying through a phonemic language, early testing for phonological (including phonemic) awareness is beneficial. Children who are aware that words consist of smaller units (syllables and phonemes) are more likely to be good readers. Reading skills correlate very strongly with student achievement. Phonological awareness can be taught in both languages of instruction. By testing for it in the first years of school, early interventions can be organised where needed before a student falls far behind his or her peers.

Taking a whole-school and home-school approach to helping students in difficulty

Early intervention is central to helping a student in difficulty before the gap between her or him and the others widens. If a student is in serious difficulty, all the teachers involved (or a special team in the case of class teachers) can meet to first identify the child's needs and to build a common strategy for meeting them. In addition, parents may require assistance in developing strategies that can support student learning. See the section on *Parents*, page 100.

Stakeholder-centred approach

Exploring topics of interest to students

Students' interests can be explored and built on in learning activities. By connecting learning to ideas and topics that are of interest to students, new learning is likely to be more meaningful.

Allowing some time every day for students to take the lead in L2 dialogue

This helps reveal the language students do not know and allows the teacher to provide it. This 'just-in-time' provision of language is more likely to be recalled by students than language which has been taught 'just-in-case' for possible future use.

Surveying students and parents

Surveys can be an excellent vehicle for getting feedback about effective practices and programme-related concerns, needs, wishes and interests. If these are taken into account in improving teaching and learning practices they can increase student motivation and achievement. These surveys often focus on: how the student learns best, what is currently impeding learning, what are current concerns/worries, and asking for suggestions.

Creating opportunities for students to meet peers from other bilingual schools

Students who have a chance to meet students from other schools who are in bilingual education are less likely to succumb to peer pressure from monolingual students to drop out of the bilingual programme.

Involving bilingual (L1, L2) psychologists, speech therapists, social workers and special education teachers

By being potentially sensitive to language and cultural issues, these individuals are well placed to make distinctions between language learning, content learning and cultural issues.

Personal perspectives

Students on learning through the L2

These anonymous quotes have been gathered from secondary students and graduates of bilingual programmes in North America and Europe.

"Studying History through another language was really interesting. You get to see History from a totally new perspective."

"My parents were really taken aback by the idea of me learning Maths through a second language. I wasn't. We had to work as a group, which was fun and stimulating. Learning through another language helped me a lot to learn the language, the words and expressions. It is harder, but you learn more.

This year we studied Science in English. And you know, most students actually had better marks. They understood more. That's a fact. We had to work harder at understanding. The teachers had to work harder to make sure we understood. It was more motivating."

"The bilingual classes allow us to study in a more pleasant way. We participate more in the lessons and it's not the classic situation with the teacher explaining things and us doing exercises. We were always doing projects, doing new things. We had to keep asking the teacher questions about how to proceed. We generally talked a lot and did lots of different activities. That's what I liked the most."

"It made it a lot easier to be able to study some of my subjects through Spanish when I arrived in the States. I couldn't speak much English. American kids were learning some of their subjects in Spanish with us Mexicans. At least half the day, I felt I could learn, show people what I could do."

"I now work for the government and use two languages almost every day. Immersion has opened lots of doors for me, not just professionally, but personally."

Addressing potential gender issues

Fewer boys than girls or vice versa may enrol in bilingual programmes, particularly late-entry programmes. In some contexts, there is a tendency for more boys to drop out of bilingual programmes than girls. In other contexts, more girls may drop out. The strategies and approaches suggested throughout this guide can do much to diminish differences in the engagement and retention of boys and girls in a bilingual programme. In addition, the following suggestions drawn from research may also help schools to manage gender issues.

A strategy for gender balance

It is helpful in mixed-gender schools to have a strategy for ensuring a gender balance upon programme intake and graduation. This strategy might include:

- openly stating that 50% of the intake will consist of girls and 50% of boys

- considering (as an analytic exercise) boys and girls as separate but equal stakeholder groups so that each group's learning needs are explored and programme advertising reviewed to make sure the interests of each group are taken into account

- exploring one's own attitudes, language and behaviour to make certain that the messages reaching parents and students about bilingual education are free of gender bias

- maintaining statistics on student drop-out and graduation rates according to gender.

Addressing imbalances

In some contexts some school subjects are perceived as more appropriate for boys or girls, and this can influence student achievement. For example, according to the World Economic Forum's Gender Gap Index (level of equality between men and women), in countries where the gender gap is small, boys and girls tend to have similar test scores in Mathematics. The opposite is the case in countries with a large gender gap. In response to concerns regarding gender, bilingual programmes can monitor the engagement and achievement of boys and girls, and develop strategies for addressing imbalances.

Learning materials

When creating learning materials, teachers are advised to ensure that boys and girls are represented equally and that they both play leadership roles. Adults depicted in teacher-created materials should reflect the realities and diversity of society, and not simply rely on stereotypes. For example, not all women are shorter than men. Furthermore, men and women hold a wide range of jobs and assume a wide variety of roles in family, and in social discourse.

Parents

In two-parent families, if both parents have high expectations for students regarding their education, discuss their school projects and plans, and celebrate their effort in learning, student achievement is likely to rise. However, researchers have noted in certain contexts that if a father leaves this responsibility to the mother, a boy may develop less of an interest in education. Likewise, if a mother does not express high expectations regarding a daughter's education, this may negatively affect the daughter's achievement.

Culture

Culture contributes to differences in the way both genders perceive the world and in the way they behave. In particular, in circumstances where students come from diverse cultural backgrounds, teachers may need support in understanding and developing strategies for dealing with cultural differences, including those that influence gender roles. For example, guided role-playing can allow students of both genders to safely explore new roles and ideas. The following are not hard and fast rules that apply to every child. They are general guidelines arising from research and teaching practice that have been found to help both genders in improving learning.

Boys (and girls)

Encourage boys to visualise or draw

Encouraging boys first to visualise something or draw a picture and then speak about the visualisation or picture usually leads to increased use of language. This counters a possible tendency in boys to use fewer words in descriptions than girls.

Provide regular opportunities to move

It is widely believed that many young male learners find it more difficult to sit still than most girls. In addition to creating opportunities for moving about the classroom and the school, teachers can direct a child's excess energy in a positive way and support concentration on learning by allowing for fidgeting or playing with pliable materials (e.g. poster tack).

Provide boys with hands-on activities

Boys tend to respond well to opportunities for hands-on activities such as experiments.

Allow young boys to use manipulatives

These might include blocks with letters on them, which can be used to build words and sentences. If students are allowed to use a digital recorder, they can record and check their own work or review how they read a text or made a presentation.

Give boys more time to process their emotions

It is thought that girls often deal with emotions more effectively than boys. In particular, boys may have more difficulty expressing themselves when they are under stress. They may need time for reflection before discussing an incident. They may find it difficult to look a teacher in the eye when discussing an emotionally intense issue. However, if there is a general perception that girls are more adept at processing their emotions, there is also a danger that girls' emotional or social difficulties may not be seen as serious enough to warrant the support girls may need to work through their difficulties.

Girls (and boys)

Provide girls with more word problems in Mathematics

As young girls may have stronger language skills than boys, this strength can be built on.

Encourage girls to explain their thinking

Girls may be less likely than boys to display their lack of knowledge to teachers. Hence, boys' learning needs may be more transparent to teachers and more likely to be quickly addressed, which can disadvantage girls.

Support girls in developing spatial-orientation skills

There is a prevalent myth that woman have innately weaker spatial-orientation skills than men. There is research to show that if women who have weaker spatial orientation skills than men are provided with the requisite short training, this gender gap can be virtually eliminated.[2]

Create additional opportunities for girls to experiment with new challenges

This can counter a possible tendency for girls to be more risk-adverse than boys.

Action research

Monitor for several lessons in a row how often and for how long boys and girls speak. If one gender speaks more often and for longer than its percentage of the class population would imply is fair, the teacher and students can discuss how to redress the balance.

---

[2]See the work of Jing Feng, Ian Spence and Jay Pratt, and of Andrea Bosco; Anna M. Longoni and Tomaso Vecchi.

5 Teachers

This chapter focuses on:

- identifying needed competences
- finding new teachers
- keeping teachers
- fostering professional development
- working with assistant teachers.

Introduction

Teachers have been referred to as the 'salt of the earth', 'the midwives of society' and those who 'teach all other professions'. They retain those roles in bilingual education. However, bilingual education does place some additional demands on teachers and students. Above all, owing to the challenges of learning through an additional language, many aspects of good pedagogy such as the scaffolding of learning require enhanced and more subtle application. Teachers in bilingual programmes require an extra set of qualifications, traits and skills. Moreover, those teaching through the L2 will have an impact on those teaching through the L1 and vice versa. As it is often a challenge in bilingual education to find and keep qualified teachers, experienced school principals suggest that the following multiple factors and strategies be taken into account.

Identifying needed competences

Language requirements

Language proficiency

Teachers require a good command of the additional language of instruction. Even if a teacher has strong social-language skills, it cannot be assumed that he or she is proficient in academic language. Principals who do not speak the additional language of instruction with a high degree of fluency are advised to seek help in assessing teachers' academic language skills.

Fluency of L2

It is helpful (but definitely not necessary) to have at least two native or otherwise highly fluent speakers of the L2 on the staff. The native or fluent speakers help provide authentic language to students. They can also support less fluent teachers of the L2 in correcting their materials and otherwise developing their L2 skills. If these native or otherwise fluent L2 speakers take on the responsibility of systematically supporting other staff, this would need to be reflected in a somewhat reduced teaching load. It is also essential that these individuals be trained in teaching through the students' L2.

Knowledge of students' L1

Also, it is advisable for teachers to have sufficient knowledge of students' L1 to understand the students when they use their first language. This is particularly important at the start of programmes at the primary level where students respond in their L1 to teachers' L2 speech. In these circumstances, teachers restate the L1 utterance in the L2 so students can respond again using the L2. Speaking the students' L1 is also important for discussing students' learning needs with parents.

Personal qualities

Interested in learning

Teachers need to be interested in learning, as it takes years to become a skilled teacher in bilingual education.

Co-operative

Quality bilingual education calls for co-operation among teachers – for example, to set common language goals or to do cross-curricular projects. Thus, it is advantageous if teachers have a co-operative nature.

Other qualities

As bilingual education places additional demands on teachers and students, knowing about **best practices in teaching and learning** is particularly important. As a minimum, teachers need to be prepared to learn about and experiment with the following: scaffolding content and language, integrating content and language, fostering critical thinking about content and language, helping students develop learning skills, helping students to connect with speakers of the L2, and using authentic materials in authentic ways. (See *A Bilingual Education Continuum* and *CLIL Essentials* on pages 50–51 and 52–53.)

Other valuable qualities include:

- **working hard and knowing how to set priorities**
- **believing that bilingual education is suitable for all** types of students is crucial, as is having high expectations for students; low expectations usually lead to impoverished learning environments
- a willingness to work in a cross-cultural environment is essential; this includes **valuing both the students' L1 and the L2** and their respective cultures.

Competences

There are several frameworks, grids and inventories that list the competences needed by teachers in bilingual education.[1] The **teacher competences** listed in these frameworks, grids and inventories are intended to serve as goals for which to strive. They are not intended as instruments for evaluating teacher qualifications.

If teachers are **qualified to teach more than one subject,** this fosters the integration of subjects, but also gives administrators greater flexibility in timetabling.

Finding new teachers

A school with high standards for learning, and for building respectful professional relationships is likely to have an advantage in attracting good teachers. This usually goes hand-in-hand with allowing staff and students some measure of autonomy and influence.

Using contacts

- **Teachers can be asked** to encourage friends, acquaintances and colleagues who speak the L2 to consider applying for a teaching job.
- Schools can conduct a **language audit.** There may be members of staff who speak the L2 better than they think, or who could qualify to teach through the L2 with some additional training.

Teacher-training institutions and student teachers

By co-operating with a teacher-training institution, **a school can become a preferred location for student-teachers to do their practicum** (teaching

---

[1] See e.g. the Target Competences in *The European Framework for CLIL Teacher Education* (http://clil-cd.ecml.at).

practice). If a school makes a systematic effort to ensure that student-teachers feel at home, as well as learn from and enjoy their practicum, they are more likely to choose that school as a place of employment. A systematic effort requires a plan and agreements detailing ways in which student-teachers will be integrated within the school as a whole (e.g. meeting the principal at the start, middle and end of a practicum; being introduced to the school by the deputy principal; sharing of materials; meeting several staff members who share their learning).

Having student-teachers in a school is **also motivating for existing teachers** as it gives them an opportunity to share their experience with interested listeners. It also encourages school staff to think about and discuss excellence in education.

In many countries a large percentage of new teachers graduating from training institutions do not enter the teaching profession. An often-cited reason is the working conditions experienced during the practicum, primarily that schools did not appear supportive and welcoming of new staff. Thus, **co-operation with teacher-training institutions and student-teachers** is a potentially highly valuable and often under-utilised source of new staff.

Approaching qualified and former teachers

Day visits

Qualified teachers can be invited to spend a day at the school. This will help them make a more informed decision about whether to apply for a job or not. During the visit, it is important to make them feel welcome, to show that the school is supportive of and respectful towards new staff, and to demonstrate that it is serious about quality education. Visitors are encouraged to express their concerns and fears regarding bilingual education and the school in particular, so that these can be constructively addressed. If this is done, these teachers will also feel they have been listened to, and that at this school, what they think would count.

Open days

In many countries, a significant number of qualified teachers have left the profession for a variety of reasons. An open house day/morning, conducted on a day when most people do not work, can be open to parents and other members of the community, but specifically target these former teachers. Some may still have an interest in the profession. The former teachers are identified on arrival and provided with a special programme.

Other options

Paying a premium

Although not widespread as a practice, some regions pay a premium for extra qualifications such as the ability to teach through the additional language. Some regions or schools have offered to provide moving expenses to teachers coming from another community.

Sharing staff

When part-time staff are required, teachers can often be shared between schools. Two part-time positions can be advertised as one full-time job at two schools. However, it is possible that someone teaching only a few classes in a school may not have the same level of commitment to the students and the school as would a full-time staff member.

Hiring native speakers

In some regions it is possible to hire native speakers who have a teaching qualification from another country. Some regional and national agencies foster teacher exchanges. However, it is helpful if these teachers have experience in teaching students who are learning through an additional language. At the very least, these teachers will probably require training in scaffolding language and content for students learning through their L2.

Local authorities

Local authorities are often aware of planned school closures and therefore of people who may soon be seeking a new teaching job.

Retired teachers

Retired teachers from a country where the L2 is spoken are often prepared to act as teacher assistants or to teach full or part-time. Embassies can often help locate these people.

Distance learning

Robots and other distance-learning options are sometimes used. In some parts of Lapland, for example, one teacher teaches one subject to students in three schools at a time. The teacher can spend several days teaching from each school. Students all have laptop computers and the teacher can (through a video link) see and speak with students in all three schools. In South Korea, some schools are experimenting with the use of L2 robot teaching assistants. A teacher who is located in another country (e.g. the Philippines) is hired to teach through the robot that is in the Korean classroom.

Keeping teachers

Teacher pre-service training, recruitment (hiring) procedures, teacher mentoring programmes, in-service training (professional development) and school work culture are all interrelated. To help ensure that staff remain motivated and continue to teach in the bilingual programme in the long term, the following are worthy of consideration.

Supporting inexperienced teachers

Problem-solving

Inexperienced teachers (with less than five years' experience) may appear to co-operate with others, but may not ask for help even when needed. They may fear colleagues will question their competence if they expose a lack of knowledge or any weaknesses. Inexperienced teachers are the most likely to resign if they feel isolated and unsupported by other teachers and school management. Inexperienced teachers may not understand that it takes years of teaching practice to develop the skills set required in bilingual education. Building a work culture that makes it legitimate to have problems and that focuses on solving them is one of the best ways of fostering learning and keeping staff.

Entry plans

Entry plans can be used to detail how a school will help integrate new staff. Entry plans can describe how new staff will receive basic information about the school. They include arrangements for new staff to meet with and learn from existing staff about a school's work practices and ethos. In this way, entry plans can facilitate the building of new relationships. Moreover, entry plans can assign new teachers a mentor, and provide networking opportunities.

Mentors

Providing inexperienced teachers with mentors can significantly increase staff retention. It is helpful if the mentor and the inexperienced teacher have the same planning time for at least the first year. This can facilitate discussion and joint lesson planning. Some schools have been known to occasionally hire a supply teacher for a few days a year to free up mentors so they can concentrate on supporting their inexperienced colleague. In addition to engaging highly experienced staff as mentors, some teachers with only a few years' experience can rise to the challenge of mentoring. However, experienced and inexperienced mentors need training. They also deserve recognition for their work.

Personal perspectives

Teachers on principals

The following quotations have been gathered from bilingual programme teachers on several continents who state how their principals support them or undermine them.

Helpful behaviours/strategies

"My principal encouraged me and trusted me when I started doing CLIL. Most importantly, he supported me at a meeting with parents who were worried about how their children would cope with CLIL."

"We have several special planning teams for the bilingual programme."

"I used to only plan activities until my new principal insisted we begin to plan lessons with language and content outcomes. She expected us to share these outcomes with the students. She kept saying students have to be able to see, hear or touch these. They have to know what is expected of them, what they can do. It was not an easy transition. Our principal supported us in making this shift through school-wide training. The shift to planning based on outcomes has made all the difference in how the school operates. I am a better teacher. Students are achieving more. We are a better school. I feel I can try new things and even make mistakes. The principal expects everybody in the school to keep learning and to try new things."

"We do a lot of work with parents, including providing free lectures and workshops on how they can support their children's learning. The principal attends and sometimes leads these lectures and workshops. The principal has invited parent volunteers to help with both L1 and L2 reading. He is always thanking parents publicly for their contribution."

Unhelpful behaviours/strategies

"Our former principal took sides. She made supportive statements about the teachers who were against the bilingual programme. The principal never said a kind word about the bilingual programme. She didn't say a word against it. She just ignored it."

"My principal is obsessed with final examination scores. It seems nothing else counts. I think this is demotivating for the students and staff. I feel this man is taking the pleasure out of learning and teaching. Surely some middle ground could be found."

> "If a principal has not been trained in managing bilingual programmes and does not understand its needs, that person will make mistakes in timetabling, co-ordinating programming and in budget decisions. If someone believes in something, they learn everything they can about it."

> "Our principal never talks to primary school principals. This puts us in a difficult position. I think we need to co-ordinate with those schools that send us students."

> "There are very few bilingual schools in our city. We are often criticised by the other schools for 'stealing the best students' and undermining the L1. Our principal doesn't seem to be bothered by this. We live in the community. I work hard. I don't want to be criticised. I want our school to do more to explain what it does. I want us to co-operate with other schools."

> "Our principal never talks with teachers. He ignores us. When we spoke to him about this and made suggestions for improvement, our constructive feedback was not accepted. Our suggestions were not implemented. There is no point in making suggestions for improvement if they and you are ignored."

> "My principal decides everything herself. Most people don't even say anything anymore when we are convinced she is making a mistake."

New challenges

Although inexperienced teachers should not be overloaded with extra responsibilities, some new challenges such as helping to organise a school bilingual day or conference can be very motivating. They provide a learning opportunity and a chance to make a difference.

Sharing material

Sharing teaching/learning material with inexperienced teachers helps to take considerable pressure off them. It shows these teachers what experienced colleagues consider to be good materials. The sharing process is likely to lead to explanations of how these materials are used. There is a shortage of materials created for bilingual education, and teachers can become overwhelmed by adapting authentic materials or creating new materials for their students. However, developing a culture of sharing often needs to be encouraged by managers and regularly returned to as a discussion point during meetings and performance reviews.

Meeting other staff

New and inexperienced teachers can benefit from opportunities to meet with other new and inexperienced teachers with no managers present. Two schools can facilitate a meeting of these teachers. Inexperienced teachers are more likely to venture an opinion in such circumstances. Teachers attending such a meeting can identify both measures that have helped them and their additional needs. By presenting these collectively, teachers are more likely to identify real needs.

Access to training and professional development

Practice-based training

Teachers who have come from a practice-based pre-service training programme are often less likely to leave teaching, as they understand better what they will be facing.

Wide access

- **When only a small group of teachers** in a school are given access to professional development they are more likely to want to move to another school. They may feel that the current school culture does not support using the new strategies they have learned, and thus seek out a school where a larger number of colleagues are prepared to innovate.
- **Experienced teachers** who are new to teaching students through their L2 can also be considered inexperienced in bilingual education. They also require professional development opportunities, including support from colleagues who are more experienced at teaching through the students' L2. They need access to learning materials in the L2. A transition plan can be developed to think systematically through ways of helping experienced teachers to adjust to teaching students through their L2.
- **Deputy principals** often play a central role in supporting teachers. They need considerable training in doing so and opportunities to discuss their efforts with the principal.
- **L1 teachers are also trained,** even in schools that are primarily teaching through the L2, so that they and their subject(s) are not seen as old fashioned.

Budgetary resources

Professional-development opportunities are motivating for many staff members. Moreover, replacing staff is costly. In addition to the direct costs associated with replacing staff members, there are many hidden costs such as the time it takes to train new staff and the demotivating effect of high staff turnover on existing staff. Hence, it is important for schools to find the budgetary resources for professional development. If teachers are asked to pay some of the costs of professional development, those costs need to be kept to a bare minimum.

Staff satisfaction

Collecting data

By collecting data on why teachers choose to stay or leave a school, it is possible to better understand and manage the co-construction of a work culture and working conditions that encourage staff satisfaction and retention. However, considerable thought will have to be put into how to make departing teachers feel safe enough to reveal the real reasons why they are leaving. For example, it is possible for a university researcher or university graduate student to do a study covering five or more schools and provide aggregated, anonymous data to participating schools.

Motivation

- **By stating their expectations** regarding the integration of new teachers and the bilingual programme, principals are likely to build support for the programme and for those teaching in it.
- **A rewards and recognition policy** can help a school to think through how to systematically foster staff, student and other stakeholder motivation. A policy that is focused on building a professional learning community, and that takes into account and celebrates in a balanced manner the contributions of staff, students, parents and other stakeholders in the bilingual (and where applicable in the regular) programme can help motivate all concerned. In particular, it is helpful if the policy can find ways of recognising groups or entire teams for their efforts so that everyone receives sincere and merited recognition.
- **Schools that emphasise high standards in learning** and support students and staff in becoming autonomous learners, as opposed to emphasising examinations results and control, tend to be more motivating for students and teachers.

Autonomy

In the short term, highly prescribed programmes where teachers are told every day exactly what to teach and in what order can support some inexperienced teachers at the start of their teaching career. In the long term, however, highly prescriptive programmes tend to lose more teachers. This is probably because opportunities for creativity and autonomous learning are reduced. As a consequence, teacher and student motivation may decline.

Working conditions

- **Planning time.** Principals can occasionally take several classes of students for one or two lessons to watch and discuss a film, so their **teachers can be freed up to plan.**

- **Workload**. When schools cope with a shortage of teachers by increasing the workload of existing teachers, they are likely to lose more in the long term than they will gain in the short-term. Overworked teachers have less time to prepare their lessons and provide students with feedback, which can lead to a possible decline in student learning. Overworked teachers are more likely to leave the school. New teachers are less likely to join the school.
- **Balance**. Teaching in bilingual programmes can be very motivating. Motivated teachers can always find something else they could do to support student learning. If this leads to extensive periods of overwork, these teachers may need support in finding a better balance in their lives.

Staff surveys

As principals are often seen by teachers as high-powered individuals, some teachers will be careful in venturing their opinion to the principal. To find out what teachers really think, anonymous staff surveys can give valuable input. These surveys will only be taken seriously if survey results are discussed openly and constructively, and action is taken to address concerns.

Dealing with conflict

A major negative incident or experience can outweigh many positive experiences and significantly influence career-related decisions. Conflicts need to be handled with care to ensure that they are turned into positive learning experiences for all involved and that everyone's dignity remains intact. Most importantly, those involved need to believe the issue has been solved.

Trust

Trust is central to keeping staff. Trust is about predictability in the face of risk or adversity. Teachers will judge principals on how they treat people in difficult situations. Because all people are on some level vulnerable, principals will also be judged on how they treat the vulnerable. Principals are more likely to keep staff if they demonstrate that they care about individuals both personally and professionally, if they keep their word, if they place student interests first, and if they speak out to protect students, staff members and the school. These actions are central to maintaining trust.

Fostering professional development

The ever-changing nature of today's world and an ever-expanding wealth of knowledge call for lifelong learning. Professional life requires ongoing professional development. Professional development is tied very closely to school culture. In a school where teachers do not open their classroom doors to others, it is difficult to institute change and support teacher learning. By contrast, a school where classroom practice is shared with others is more likely to become a professional learning community. The diagram below shows the considerations that are often pointed to as essential for successful professional development (PD).

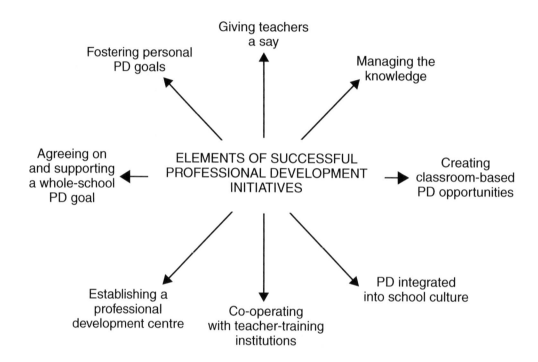

Giving teachers a say

Teachers are more likely to attend and benefit from professional-development opportunities when they have a say in what training and support they receive. In addition to expressing preferences, this would involve a discussion that is informed by student feedback and achievement data, parental feedback data, and lesson observations data.

Whole-school improvement goals

As well as encouraging teachers to establish personal goals for professional development, it is also advisable to choose one topic that is tied to a whole-school improvement goal, such as fostering greater critical thinking or building learner autonomy. The widespread focus on one such topic increases the possibility that this will benefit students.

Integrating professional development into the school culture

Content and language

The integration of content and language, and the supporting of language learning in content classes, are two challenges which often require special ongoing training in bilingual education contexts.

Access to knowledge

Providing teachers with access to knowledge from meta-studies which have analysed teaching and learning practices that have a significant impact on student learning is particularly important in a bilingual education context, where teachers and students are faced with the extra challenge of learning through two languages. This helps show teachers which teaching and learning practices can potentially bring the biggest returns. Equally importantly, knowledge about the results of research into schools of excellence can prove invaluable in structuring professional development.

Changing needs

Teachers' professional development needs change from year to year. Teachers who have successfully taught one subject or grade (year or level) through the L2 may not necessarily know how to teach another grade. For example, a teacher may know how to teach through the L2 if the concepts are easily taught through visuals, but not know how to do so when the academic content is more abstract and challenging.

Opportunities for discussion

Devoting a fixed portion of a monthly full-school meeting to professional development can help stress that a school is serious about all staff learning. Effective professional development initiatives give teachers rich opportunities to discuss their education-related understandings, beliefs and practices. Such discussions are a way of co-constructing knowledge rather than an attempt at knowledge transmission.

Classroom-based opportunities

Reflection and autonomy

Classroom-based training is thought to be much more effective than lectures. For example, a teacher can videotape a lesson and choose two five-minute clips that he or she shows others – one showing something that went well and one showing something he or she would like to improve. This gives a teacher considerable control. Central to the use of this strategy is giving teachers a say in how large a group will view and discuss these clips. Few teachers would feel comfortable having such a discussion with the entire school staff. Discussion can be focused on only one topic such as fostering learner autonomy. This again increases teacher control over what will be discussed. Other potentially effective strategies include: creating and discussing portfolios of student work (e.g. compositions) and teacher work (e.g. sample lesson plans or adapted materials); writing and analysing a diary about teaching; discussing jointly observed lessons; and presenting a mini-lesson to colleagues and then discussing it.

The walk–about support system

A five-minute walk-about support system can foster the professional development of all concerned. This system involves the principal or deputy principal (or other mentors) doing brief, semi-unannounced classroom visits. The observer looks to see if students are fully engaged in curriculum-based learning. He or she also observes classroom climate and what is displayed on classroom walls. **No criticism is made** of what is observed. Instead, during a ten-minute follow-up meeting, a supportive question or two is asked of the teacher (e.g.: 'I noticed you displayed language needed for doing group work and for discussing cell growth. How do students use this?'; 'How else do you scaffold content and language use?'; 'What criteria are you using to measure ongoing language growth?'). A professional dialogue about teaching/learning ensues.

The five-minute walk-about support system can be proposed and discussed at a meeting where teachers are reassured that the aim is to increase professional dialogue and learning, and not to identify weaknesses. Volunteers can be invited to offer an open-door policy to others. As trust is built in the constructive nature of the experience, others will want to become part of this system. Ultimately, the five-minute walk-about support system is about building a **reflective work culture**. This can help foster a school climate that is based on teachers, deputy principals and principals being focused on their own and student learning.

Lesson observation

It is advisable to give teachers a say in lesson observation processes and in deciding on criteria or 'look-fors' for analysing those lessons of theirs that are observed by others. This will give them a greater sense of control over and interest in the observation process and follow-up discussion. It will also probably increase the possibility that the lesson observation and discussion process will contribute to improvements in teaching practices. It should help to ensure that observation and discussion are a positive experience for all concerned and that they support the professional development of all those involved.

A professional development policy

A professional development policy created in co-operation with staff can help a school get the most out of professional development.

Primary and supporting goals

A **primary goal** of the professional development policy can be that it seeks to serve the interest of students and lead to an improvement in their content and language achievement. A two-page policy might also include supporting goals, values, stakeholders, guiding principles, and success indicators. For example, **supporting goals** could include: to articulate a common understanding of supportive and effective learning environments; and to define the skills and competences required by professional development participants, as well as related needs and activities. These would support participants' engagement in learning.

Success indicators

Professional development policy success indicators might include: the extent to which learning from training sessions is applied in classrooms; and student achievement and development. These are measured, among others, through lesson observations, surveys and student achievement tests. This will help ensure that the success of professional development initiatives are not simply measured by participants' satisfaction levels, but that the focus is on improving teaching and learning. In addition, by identifying deputy principals, assistant teachers, parents, support staff, and other stakeholders, a policy can help an entire school become a professional learning community.

Co-operating with teacher-training institutions

Some schools who receive student teachers co-operate closely with the teacher-training institution. This is an opportunity for professional dialogue and a way of accessing new ideas. On a practical level this can involve having supervising teachers and teacher trainers meet during student-teacher placements for a weekly debriefing session at the school. Sometimes student teachers attend these sessions.

Establishing a professional development centre

A school can become a professional development centre that runs bilingual education conferences or professional development days for staff members, parents and educators from other schools. When teaching others, people have to be able to summarise what they do. In addition, training others motivates those doing the training to learn new and better ways of building quality learning environments. Running a bilingual education conference is a good starting point for putting one's expertise on show and for learning from others.

Managing knowledge

Knowledge from professional development programmes needs to be managed and made easily accessible to all staff members in one central location such as the school's intranet site. In addition, a school can purchase books about teaching/learning in bilingual education and subscribe to bilingual education journals. Equally importantly, books and journals about best practice in education in general can be provided. Once a month at a staff meeting, one or more teachers can present a book review or salient points from a journal article.

 Personal perspective

Supporting professional development

Conrad Hughes (International School of Geneva) is the Director of Education for eight schools that foster different forms of strong integrative bilingual learning. He suggests:

Building belief

Senior staff drive the bilingual programme and the first thing to be sure of is that they believe in the cognitive, social and cultural benefits of this type of educational provision.

To ensure that senior staff are prepared to support teachers, we try to expose them to research and literature on the subject. We meet with them to make sure that a common understanding can be developed about pedagogy and to ensure that senior staff are prepared to champion a learning programme about which they are passionate and enthusiastic.

Language responsibility

Even teachers teaching through the L1 need to think about the fact that language is a vehicle for learning as a basic attribute of good pedagogy. We help them to remain reflective about the way they use language to clarify concepts and communicate ideas.

A rich environment

Bilingual learning implies bilingual resources ranging from books on the theory of bilingual learning and journal subscriptions to texts in the languages being taught. The librarian reaches the school community regularly through staff meetings and online.

Tapping into talent

This could include speakers at inset professional development days as well as non-teaching members of the school community (e.g. administrative staff) whose language of communication could be used in creative ways to support bilingualism. A dynamic response to the challenge of creating a successful bilingual learning project would be using lateral support and energy in creative ways that go beyond the classroom.

Working with assistant teachers

Many bilingual schools have assistant teachers, language assistants or volunteers in the classroom with the teacher. As teachers are used to teaching on their own, it is quite possible that they will need support from school management in effectively using this resource. Teachers can be supported in developing a professional partnership with assistant teachers when school managers engage with teachers and assistant teachers. This can be achieved in the following ways:

- **Planning.** The assistant teacher participates in planning the lesson and in assessing students. The teacher carries final responsibility for planning and assessment. However, by participating in both of these activities the assistant teacher is likely to approach his or her work more thoughtfully, and be more motivated.

- **L2 model.** Assistant teachers play an important role in providing students with another L2 language model, and thus need rich opportunities to interact with students.

- **Accessibility.** The assistant teacher is given opportunities to work with all types of students in the classroom, not just those in difficulty.

- **Status.** Assistant teachers participate in meetings with parents. Although assistant teachers can discipline students, they are not meant to constantly sit only with students who have difficulty in disciplining themselves.

- **Small-group dialogue.** Assistant teachers can foster the use of dialogue in teaching, critical thinking and learning-skills development. For example, they can work with a small group to discuss how to solve a problem or do an assignment. They can help build context, and have students suggest several possible ways of solving the problem or doing the assignment. These student suggestions can then be analysed and one solution can be chosen. The assistant teacher can help students plan for how to do their work, how to get the help they need and how to find and use new learning strategies.

- **Whole class.** Assistant teachers can also lead whole-class activities such as brainstorming the language students might need to write a story.

Personal perspective

Recognising and navigating complexities

In addition to Estonian-medium schools, Estonia has many Russian-medium schools serving mostly the children of Russian-speakers who moved to Estonia during the Soviet era. Valeri Novikov is the principal of one of these schools, which also happens to be one of the largest in the country. Over ten years ago, he directed the launch of an Estonian-language immersion programme beginning in Grade 1 in his Russian-language school. Valeri Novikov says:

I recognised some years ago that our students needed to learn to speak Estonian in order to integrate into Estonian society and be successful. It was clear that we had to do something to help our students learn Estonian better and more quickly. Consequently, when the opportunity presented itself, our school competed with many others to join the national immersion programme. We won entry into the programme and I remain pleased with my decision to embark down the road of developing a multilingual school.

Initially, I imagined that I needed only to hire a teacher and the programme would run itself. Now I understand that introducing an immersion programme is a complex process that requires the involvement of the entire school staff. It also **requires co-operation** with parents, local government, the Ministry of Education and Research, international partners and other immersion schools. It is a time-consuming but rewarding process.

Study visits to Canada and Finland were immensely useful in helping all participants understand how best to introduce and manage such programmes. Equally importantly, opportunities for dialogue with colleagues from other schools introducing immersion in Estonian have been invaluable. There is so much to learn from one another within Estonia and from abroad. Having an agency that co-ordinates programme development nationally has been an enormous help in **facilitating the exchange of information** and the management of knowledge about teaching and learning in bilingual schools.

Moreover, the immersion programme requires **special teachers**. Not only must teachers speak Estonian fluently, they also need to be prepared to work in a different way and be open to new ideas and methodologies. Teachers in immersion programmes have to work hard. They need a sense of mission.

It is also unrealistic to expect one immersion teacher to be the embodiment of the entire Estonian language and culture. It is important to **support**

opportunities where children can speak to and **get to know other Estonians**. In recognition of this, and of the fact the immersion teachers have a heavy workload, we have supported our teachers by hiring part-time assistant teachers.

It is essential for the school to support the immersion teacher by raising the **profile and status of the programme** in the school. Much work needs to be done with the rest of the staff in the school to ensure that the immersion programme is welcomed. Some of our teachers were concerned that this new programme could place their jobs at risk. Since many Russian-speaking parents are placing their children in Estonian schools, I actually see immersion as a way of retaining enrolment in Russian-language schools.

As well, the school has worked closely with parents so they can best understand how to support their children who are in the programme. We have also had to work hard with the press to **dispel misconceptions** about immersion. The programme does not seek to assimilate anyone, as a few uninformed journalists have speculated. On the contrary, we are looking to enrich our students by giving them additional language skills.

Having over more than ten years seen and spoken to the children and parents in this programme, and having positive examinations results, it is clear that **immersion is a success**. I know we made the right decision in offering this programme. Moreover, the early immersion programme has helped us prepare for introducing a form of late immersion to ensure that all children in the school have access to enriched language-learning opportunities.

6 Parents

This chapter focuses on:

- gaining and maintaining support
- addressing parental concerns
- helping parents to support students
- involving non-programme parents.

Introduction

Well-informed parents or guardians (henceforth parents) are central to the success of bilingual programmes. This is because there is often a direct link between parental understandings/attitudes/actions and student achievement. In addition, parents can support a programme and in so doing help to make it successful; or if they are against the idea, they can consciously or unconsciously work to oppose it.

Gaining and maintaining support

Decisions are made on both an intellectual and an emotional level. This means that parents, as well as wanting factual information about bilingual education, also seek reassurance that bilingual programmes are respected by people in the community such as government officials and academics. Perhaps most importantly, though, parents tend to trust other parents. Therefore, prospective bilingual-programme parents find it helpful to hear from other parents whose children have already been in a bilingual programme.

Prior to entering the programme

The following measures have been found to help parents and/or students to make an informed decision about joining a bilingual programme.

Special classes

A special class can be offered to children at the kindergarten level, or with older students after school one day a week, to help them warm to the idea of learning through an L2. Sometimes older students are offered **a two-week module** taught through the L2 within an existing school subject. This is done in the year before students would start in the programme. This allows the students to get to know the teacher(s) and to enjoy success in learning through the L2.

Introductory meetings

Parents can be invited to an introductory meeting that includes information from the **principal, deputy principal, teachers teaching through the L2** and those teaching through the L1, and the school psychologist. This builds confidence in those attending the meeting by showing that the programme enjoys a broad base of support in the school.

Parents can gain additional information about and **confidence** in the programme if local government officials and experts from a university also attend the introductory meeting. Also, parents whose children have been in the programme, even if they are from another school, can be invited to attend. If the programme is designed for older students, it is helpful to include students who have several years' experience in the programme.

During the **typical introductory meeting**:

- A short overview is provided of programme goals and plans.
- An overview of key research findings about bilingual education is shared (see pages 18–20).
- Each speaker shares his or her perspective on the programme.
- The majority of time is given to questions from parents (and students in the case of late-entry programmes). Attendees are encouraged to express their fears and concerns so that they can be addressed. (See *Addressing parental concerns*, page 103.)

Over-optimistic descriptions of bilingual education **will not build trust** in the programme. In addition to explaining programme benefits, it is important to be open and frank about programme challenges. For example, students will have to work harder, content learning may be temporarily restricted at the start of the programme while students develop their language skills, and it is difficult to always find enough qualified teachers.

Parents will want to know that **teachers are trained** for the programme, and that the school is **co-operating with other schools**.

At the **end of the meeting**, parents and students are told that they are welcome to stay and ask questions individually of any of the speakers. This will give those parents who may have felt uncomfortable speaking in front of others an opportunity to ask their questions. It also shows that school staff are accessible to parents.

A **written overview** of programme goals and plans can also be provided to the parents, along with a registration form (see pages 2–3, 25).

A student's initial years in the programme

The first year

During the first year of the programme it is suggested that at least four **meetings** be held with parents. Parents will often ask the same questions from one meeting to the next. They are simply seeking reassurance. Once their comfort level with the programme rises, their questions will change.

A **letter** can be sent home once a month electronically or in hard copy explaining what the students are learning. It can include a monthly suggestion on how parents can support their child in learning. It can also include a list of L2 phrases that are currently being used at school and that parents may be interested in learning and using in speaking with their child.

Retaining support in the second and third years

After initial enthusiasm for the programme, support for it may drop in the second and third year. This change in support may go unnoticed if the school does not develop a culture of listening to and surveying parents. Researchers often find a gulf between how well schools think they are doing in working with parents and what parents actually think. Regaining and holding onto parental support will be more difficult than steadily working at maintaining it from the start.

Celebrating short-term wins

As language learning takes years, it is important to help parents see and celebrate their child's short-term wins or accomplishments. Short-term wins help draw out the steps of the language-learning process, which can include: students' understanding of spoken L2 speech; writing their first L2 composition or pattern-based small storybook; writing up experiments; and a successful inter-school project. It is also important to highlight what remains to be learned. By making both short-term wins and future planned learning visible, parents will be better placed to judge what has been and still needs to be accomplished.

Continued study

In addition to focusing on their children's current learning and well-being, parents will want to know what options are available for continued study through the L2 in the next stages of their child's education.

Managing visits

A monthly visitors' day can be created when parents know they are welcome to attend classes and to discuss the experience with staff. As students become older, opportunities could also be created for parents to speak with students during the visitors' day.

Encouraging L2 use

Parents can be encouraged to facilitate some in-home and otherwise out-of-school L2 use. (See *Helping parents to support students*, page 106.)

Addressing parental concerns

Parents in bilingual programmes are often more active than those in primarily monolingual programmes. Parents need plenty of opportunities to express their understandings and concerns. Moreover, as several aspects of bilingual education are counter-intuitive, it is important for schools regularly to share knowledge from research with parents. This increases the possibility that they will make well-informed decisions regarding the programme.

Communicating with parents

Educational goals

If parents are asked over several years to discuss with the school their language, content and learning-skills goals for their child, they are more likely to reflect on their child's education and their own role in supporting it.

Accessibility to the school and its staff

It is helpful for parents to know whom to approach, for which issues, at what times, and using which media. This would include ensuring that the principal's, deputy principal's and the teachers' office hours and contact numbers are made available. To facilitate electronic communication, each member of staff can have an email address, and a special Skype address such as their full name followed by the name of the school. This information can be made available on a school website and in home–school meetings. In addition, home–school meeting dates can be announced well in advance to ensure parents can fit them into their schedule. Schools can also ask parents for their preferred channels of communication. Staff accessibility is a key factor used by parents when judging a school.

Managing expectations

Unless parents are made aware of the typical learning cycle for both content and language in the bilingual programme, they may have unrealistic expectations. For example, in intensive total early-immersion programmes, students' L1 writing performance will be comparable to that of students in L1 monolingual programmes within a few years of receiving instruction through the L1. Although content knowledge (e.g. in Mathematics and Science) may initially be somewhat restricted at the start of learning through the L2, this is temporary. In the long term, students in quality bilingual programmes learn as much content as students in monolingual programmes. When parents understand these issues, they are less likely to pressure the school about them or remove their child from the programme. Realistic expectations also need to be developed regarding the final outcomes that a programme can hope to achieve. Language learning is a lifelong process. Students graduating from a bilingual programme are unlikely to be as fluent in their L2 as the average native speaker of that language. They will, however, probably be able to continue to study through the L2 and seek employment where they are required to use the L2.

Commonly asked questions

- **Is the programme only meant for high achievers?** (See page 19.)
- **Can my child easily move back to a monolingual programme, if they find the bilingual programme too difficult?** There is no reason to assume that a student's problems would be resolved by moving to a monolingual programme. It is normally recommended that students stay in the programme and be given extra help. The extra stimulation of learning through an L2 can have a positive impact on learning in general. Moreover, students may feel a sense of failure upon leaving the programme.
- **How can I help my child, if I do not speak the L2?** Ultimately, students need to learn for themselves. Moreover, having a parent who does not speak the L2 carries with it several potential benefits for the child. First, a child needs to use his or her L1 to explain to the parent what he or she has been learning. Next, the child has to explain what it is that he or she does not understand. These are two cognitively demanding tasks. Hence, they are likely to foster learning. Moreover, the act of 'translanguaging' (in this case switching from using the language of schooling to using the L1 at home, in order to work through one and the same topic or concept) and discussion with a patient parent may help deepen a child's understanding of the topic or concept, and foster both L1 and L2 development. Parents can also support a child in developing learning strategies. Since the child will need to 'translanguage' once again to finish an assignment in the L2 or apply the concept using the L2 in the classroom, this builds learner autonomy and makes it less likely that the parent will do a child's work or thinking for him/her.
- **Will L1 competence suffer?** (See pages 18–19.)
- **Will my child learn less Maths and Science?** (See pages 18–19.)

- **What language will the school-leaving examination be in, and will my child be prepared to take the exam in this language?** These are questions that some parents ask when their children enter the first grade. Some schools and education systems allow students to write their examinations in either language of instruction. Others have the students take examinations in the language used to study a given subject.

- **Will my child be disadvantaged if after graduation he or she studies at a vocational school or university teaching through the L1?** Bilingually educated students are more likely to be sensitive to language in general, and hence have an advantage in reading and writing in their L1.

- **Will my child lose touch with his or her L1 culture?** In additive bilingual education contexts this is extremely unlikely to occur. In additive contexts, hours of exposure to the student's L1 remain considerably higher than in-school exposure to the L2. In contexts where the L2 is gaining an ever-increasing presence in society including in the workplace, at cultural events, in higher education and in day-to-day social discourse, considerable effort needs to be made to ensure that the L1 is protected and used in a wide range of contexts.[1]

Other concerns

Providing a safety-net

Parents will want to know that the bilingual programme will not turn into an experience where their children will be left on their own to succeed or fail. Explaining how students in the programme are supported, and making transparent procedures for early identification of problems and the ways in which they will be addressed, will build parental confidence.

Knowing what *not* to do

For example, parents can be encouraged not to re-teach in the L1 everything that has been learnt through the L2 and not to ask children to provide simultaneous interpretation of an L2 television programme. In addition, parents need to avoid projecting their own fears about learning through an L2 onto their children.

A parents' bilingual education association

Powerful parent groups (e.g. Canadian Parents for French) have developed in some countries, which lobby for improved bilingual education opportunities and raise awareness about the phenomenon. Parents may need support in registering and launching such an organisation.

---

[1]See the work of Joshua Fishman on language shift.

Helping parents to support students

'Like parent, like child' is a saying that to some extent is backed up by educational research. Parents can benefit from being helped to see the link between their actions and attitudes and their child's success. The following are some of the ways in which bilingual schools can better harness the power of parental understandings, attitudes, actions and traditions in support of student learning.

Encouraging communication between schools and parents

Early years

Teachers can meet with nursery school parents to encourage them to use L2 nursery rhymes and songs even before their children enter the bilingual programme. The way in which parents work with the school is often set in the early years of a child's education.

Positivity

Parents can be advised to speak positively and constructively about the bilingual programme, the teachers and the school. Parental attitudes regarding the programme, the teachers and the school have a direct and often deep impact on student learning.

Rapid intervention based on thorough analysis

Parents can be encouraged **not to assume** that if a child is having difficulty understanding something at school, the **problem is the language**. A child may simply need help in understanding and linking concepts. Parents can be invited to contact the teacher, deputy principal or principal as soon as they notice a problem. In this way, the problem can be analysed and dealt with before it becomes bigger and more difficult to handle, and before it negatively affects anyone's attitude or seriously undermines the student's self-confidence.

Information and scaffolding for home-school co-operation

Parents may not know what to speak about and how to communicate with the school. They can be given a **glossary of key terms** such as core curriculum concepts associated with student learning and acronyms that are often used in conversations at your school. An **overview** of the various vehicles used for home-school dialogue can be provided. In addition, parents can be offered **information (discussion) sessions** about topics such as: how to work with the teacher, how to get the most out of meetings with teachers (or out of parent–teacher–student meetings), and how to support their children in becoming engaged readers. A **lending library** can be created of articles, guides, videos and books about how parents can support student learning and co-operate with the school.

Laying foundations for successful reading

Since one of the strongest indicators of **student achievement** is the extent to which students are **engaged readers**, parents can do much to lay the foundations for successful reading.

L1 family reading

Family reading time can be made into a family tradition. For example, parents can read to younger children in their L1 and turn it into an interactive experience, asking questions and speaking about the reading selection and related illustrations. Books can be re-read and discussed again. Eventually students can be asked to read short passages to parents. With total early L2 immersion programmes, it is particularly important for parents to read and discuss children's stories in the L1 about the L1 culture and traditions. As L1 reading skills are transferable from one language to another, by reading with their child in their L1 parents are supporting both learning through the L1 and the L2.

L1 books in library

In addition to providing parents with access to information (discussion) sessions as suggested above, each classroom can begin to develop a lending library with recommended L1 books. Parents can be encouraged to donate books to the library.

Developing oral and aural language skills

Meaningful parent–child communication

It is helpful for parents to know that children in bilingual programmes with good L1 skills often develop good L2 skills. In addition to fostering reading in the L1, families can develop the habit of **discussing a wide variety of topics**. Strong oral language skills build self-esteem and the ability to make friends. Researchers have found that high self-esteem and good social skills have a positive influence on a person's ability to learn.

School can be considered as a child's first job and a highly meaningful experience. Parents can support children's learning by showing an active interest in it, for example, by asking the child to teach them once a week a new word in the L2. Demonstrating an active interest might also involve not asking: 'How was school today?' 'What did you learn?'. Instead parents can first show they are glad to see their child and make small talk. Parents can speak about their own day. Children may then be more likely to speak about their day. Parents can ask specific questions such as: 'Which friends did you speak to today?' 'Did something funny happen today?' 'What did Mr Wong speak about in History class today?' Schools can further support discussions in the home by letting parents know once a week what themes are being explored at school. Finally, instead of suggesting plans and solutions to problems, parents can be encouraged to ask their children **guiding questions** so they can explore solutions together.

L2 resources and events

Parents can be advised to borrow L2 children's books from the library, purchase L2 books, find children's L2 programmes on television or the internet, listen to music by artists who sing in the L2, and attend events taking place in the L2. Researchers have found, however, that parents often want help in selecting books, games and internet sites. L2 recorded books are particularly popular with parents and students.

Contact and communication with L2 speakers

Students can join amateur sports teams that operate in the L2. One major study has found a strong link between students' L2 skills and the number of times per year parents arrange for their children to attend events in the L2.

Increasing parental and family involvement

Meetings and planning exercises

Parents can be invited to set part of the agenda for school meetings. This shows the school is serious about listening to parents and partnership. They can also be asked for input during programme planning and evaluation exercises. They can be encouraged to identify their children's and the community's needs, and to always be constructive during discussions. The focus is best maintained on solutions and avoiding blame. It is also important for parents to **avoid drawing regular comparisons** between their children and students studying through the L1.

Family activities

During school holidays, several schools and groups of schools have organised **language camps for families**. At these, parents are provided with content and L2 language-learning activities. Parents are also offered L1 lectures and discussion forums on bilingual education. Students have their own programme where the L2 is used in, for example, art, orienteering, swimming or skiing activities. Several L2 activities are also organised for the whole family.

During the academic year, schools can organise language **classes for parents**. As parents are busy people, however, they may have trouble finding the time to attend these classes. Taking this into account, some schools and regions have experimented with offering parents music, photography or other classes through the L2 in order to give them an authentic opportunity to use both content and language.

In addition, an **activity bag** can be sent home with young learners once a month. The bag contains learning activities that children are asked to do with their families. Also parents can act as chaperones on **field trips** or where possible to offer their workplace as a field-trip site. Also, **parents, grandparents, aunts, uncles and family friends** who speak the school's L2 as a first language can be invited to come to the school to teach folktales or dances, to talk about L2 traditions or other topics, or in later years to speak about how the L2 has served them in their personal or professional lives.

Working with parents of adolescents

Special effort may need to be expended in order to keep parents of adolescents involved with the school and their children's education. Adolescence is a particularly challenging time. Adolescents whose parents attend school functions and who volunteer at a school often have higher achievement rates than those adolescents whose parents do not do so. Parents may need to be reminded that discussing and praising effort and learning-skills development is generally more effective than praising achievement. Parents can be encouraged to develop the habit of listening to their children explain how they plan and execute their school projects. Family communication seminars can be of help.

Involving non–programme parents

If a school has both a bilingual and a regular primarily monolingual programme, it is important to ensure that parents of both programmes know something about and support the other programme. In addition, regular-programme parents will want to know:

- that their children are getting **an equal share** of the school's attention and resources
- how the school will provide their children with some **added value** through, for example, a special Mathematics initiative or a rich extra-curricular programme: the bilingual programme will be seen to provide extra value, and this will create a similar expectation regarding the regular programme
- that their children will be afforded **special language-learning opportunities** such as the provision of short CLIL modules, or the possibility of participating in a student-exchange programme with a school using the L2 as a medium of instruction.

7 Conclusion

Bilingual education holds the promise of value-added education. A diverse range of students stand to not only become bilingual and biliterate – a highly valuable set of skills in itself – but to gain access to a much wider range of benefits in life. In turn, society, whether locally, regionally, nationally or internationally, has much to gain.

Yet bilingual education is not for the faint-hearted – not that education ever is. The complexities of leading, managing, teaching and learning in these programmes are numerous. Above all, those working in bilingual education need to be prepared to learn, listen, co-operate and grow. Even if much is known about effective strategies for implementing bilingual programmes, no formulaic solutions can be applied. Still, knowledge about implementing programming is an important foundation piece. This guide has sought to provide some of that knowledge-base.

By seeking to take into account the large number of potential variables that can influence bilingual education, a principal can build his or her capacity to manage the expected and the probable. In this way, it is possible to reduce contingency and risk. Principals ideally operate both at an overarching macro level, as well as at the micro level, always balancing the big picture against important details. Furthermore, having a strong knowledge-base about bilingual education builds a principal's credibility and capacity to lead.

As the complexities of teaching in and leading and implementing bilingual programmes originate to a large extent in the multiple perceptions, understandings and actions of stakeholders, it is particularly important for principals to build their capacity to lead stakeholder learning and co-operation. Using their knowledge-base about bilingual education, principals are called on to navigate their own context in thoughtful ways. Above all, this involves understanding, synthesising and navigating the diversity and commonalities inherent in individual views, procedures, organisations and systems at large, while being able to influence and support stakeholder learning and co-constructed change at all those levels. Ultimately, bilingual education is a co-operative endeavour.

Afterword

Peeter Mehisto's lucid and timely *Excellence in Bilingual Education: A Guide for School Principals* addresses an important gap in the literature on bilingual education. As he documents, we have abundant research evidence that well-implemented bilingual programmes can develop fluency and literacy in L1 and L2 among students from both dominant and non-dominant language backgrounds. However, relatively little attention has been devoted to what constitutes 'well-implemented' bilingual education. This book specifies what policy-makers and school administrators need to know and do in order to ensure that bilingual programmes achieve their goals.

There are multiple complexities in bilingual and multilingual school contexts that can affect the implementation of any bilingual programme. These complexities range from ensuring that teachers have the appropriate linguistic competencies required to deliver effective instruction in each language, to addressing socio-political issues related to the status of the languages in the wider society and, by extension, in the school itself. Thus, the implementation of effective bilingual programmes requires ongoing collegial dialogue and professional development among the entire school staff, including the school principal. Effective bilingual instruction is not just a matter of taking the mainstream school curriculum and delivering it through two languages. There is a knowledge-base with respect to bilingual instruction that is constantly being updated as bilingual programmes expand into new geographical and social spheres and as classroom research casts light on what constitutes effective practice in different contexts. Thus, Mehisto's suggestion that approximately every two years school staff revisit their policies and practices with respect to L1 and L2 use represents extremely useful advice.

This shifting reality with respect to effective practice can be illustrated with reference to one of the defining axioms of French immersion programmes in Canada, which was articulated by Wallace Lambert (1984), whose evaluation of the initial immersion programme in the area of St Lambert near Montreal was immensely influential in legitimising bilingual education (Lambert and Tucker, 1972). Lambert, together with most other researchers and policy-makers in the

Canadian context in the 1970s and 1980s, considered it axiomatic that each language should be kept rigidly separate, even to the extent of pretending to students that the French-medium teacher knew no English. In the following quote, he clearly expressed the monolingual instructional philosophy underlying early French immersion programmes (1984, page 13):

> *No bilingual skills are required of the teacher, who plays the role of a monolingual in the target language ... and who never switches languages, reviews materials in the other language, or otherwise uses the child's native language in teacher–pupil interactions. In immersion programs, therefore, bilingualism is developed through two separate monolingual instructional routes.*

This 'two solitudes' assumption is currently being re-examined in both Canadian and international bilingual education contexts. There is certainly a rationale for creating largely separate spaces for each language within a bilingual or immersion programme. However, this goal is not at all incompatible with the implementation of bilingual instructional strategies designed to achieve certain pedagogical goals that are less easily achieved through monolingual instructional strategies. Specifically, there are compelling arguments to be made for teaching for transfer across languages (Cummins, 2007). The reality is that students are making cross-linguistic connections throughout the course of their learning in a bilingual or L2 immersion programme, so why not nurture this learning strategy and help students to apply it more efficiently? An unfortunate consequence of rigid adherence to the two solitudes assumption in bilingual and immersion education is that teachers are unable to draw students' attention to the rich cognate relationships that exist across languages such as English and French. Teachers are also likely to be constrained in encouraging students to showcase their growing bilingual and biliteracy skills and accomplishments through the writing and web-publishing of bilingual stories or projects because these endeavours entail connecting and translating across the two languages, which violates the two solitudes assumption.

As school principals lead their teachers and other school staff in collegial dialogue focused on excellence in bilingual education, it might be useful to emphasise that bilingual education entails pedagogical possibilities or 'affordances' that go beyond what is typically available within a monolingual school context. As noted above, greater awareness of how language works can be developed through drawing students' attention to cognate relationships across languages and encouraging students to compare and contrast their two languages. For example, the fact that French distinguishes between *tu* and *vous* to signify the nature of interlocutors' relationship can be used to highlight the fact that these relationships are not formally marked in English. Typically, native

English-speaking students in a monolingual English programme never become aware of this sociolinguistic feature of the English language. They simply take it for granted. By contrast, students in a French–English bilingual programme will become aware of this feature of English by virtue of the contrast with French.

Recent technological advances associated with the internet open up additional pedagogical affordances within bilingual programmes. For example, linguistic, inter-cultural and academic enrichment can result from sister-class connections where students in bilingual programmes carry out projects in both languages in collaboration with a geographically distant group of peers. To illustrate, students in Spanish–English bilingual programmes in the United States and Mexico might engage in a sister-class project that explores the origins of revolutions in society, focusing on both the American and Mexican revolutions which are part of their respective social-studies curricula. Through this kind of cross-cultural bilingual project, students will receive considerably more authentic oral and written input in their weaker language from their sister-class peers and they are also likely to use this language for intellectual inquiry considerably more than when classroom instruction focuses only on transmitting the curriculum. Students' collaborative work can be published in both languages on their respective schools' websites. By contrast, in a monolingual sister-class exchange (e.g. English-speaking students in Canada connecting with students in the United Kingdom), the process, while valuable, is likely to be considerably less culturally and linguistically enriching because only one language is involved.

Thus, as Peeter Mehisto points out in his concluding remarks, bilingual programmes hold the promise of value-added education. In order to highlight these value-added possibilities, it might be fruitful for educators in bilingual programmes to shift from a discourse of implementing *effective* instruction to a discourse of implementing *inspirational* instruction. The former entails the connotation of simply meeting the challenge of delivering the mainstream curriculum through two languages, whereas the latter highlights explicitly the possibilities for enrichment – inter-cultural, intellectual, and linguistic – that extend beyond what is typically envisaged within a mainstream monolingual programme. Inspirational pedagogy aspires to much more than simple transmission of curriculum content. Rather, the goal is to involve students in active inquiry and generation of knowledge. In addition, inspirational pedagogy implemented in bilingual programmes will engage students in producing literature, art, dramatic performances, videos or multimedia projects in both their languages, and in publishing their work for a wider audience through the internet. Students whose intellectual and personal identities are being affirmed through this kind of challenging and creative academic work are much more likely to take ownership of their two languages than is the case when the languages are used only for transmission of a static curriculum.

Thus, the value-added possibilities within bilingual programmes derive not just from the development of fluency in an additional language at no cost to students' proficiency in their L1. In a more fundamental sense, the true value of any bilingual programme can be gauged with reference to what students *do* with their two languages both within and outside the classroom. In this regard, I would argue that the potential of any bilingual programme will only be realised when the school focuses on implementing inspirational pedagogy. Inspirational pedagogy within bilingual programmes will include the production of *identity texts* (Cummins and Early, 2011) in two languages, thereby affirming students' growing sense of themselves as capable of using their languages powerfully in a wide range of social and geographical contexts. The term *identity texts* describes the products of students' creative work or performances carried out within the pedagogical space orchestrated by the classroom teacher. Students invest their identities in the creation of these texts which can be written, spoken, signed, visual, musical, dramatic, or combinations in multi-modal form. The identity text then holds a mirror up to students in which their identities are reflected back in a positive light. Students who share identity texts with multiple audiences (peers, teachers, parents, grandparents, sister classes, the media, and so on) are likely to receive positive feedback and affirmation of self in interaction with these audiences. Creation of bilingual identity texts is likely to result in affirmation that students are linguistically talented as well as accomplished in multiple additional ways. Although not always an essential component, technology acts as an amplifier to enhance the process of identity-text production and dissemination.

The title of this volume – *Excellence in Bilingual Education* – is apt. The focus of research over the past 40 years has been on 'proof of concept' – showing that instruction through two languages can develop strong L2 skills at no cost to L1. We are now shifting to the issue of *excellence* – how to implement bilingual programmes in ways that will maximise students' learning and intellectual development in both their languages. By synthesising the knowledge-base so clearly, Peeter Mehisto has provided a conceptual foundation for ongoing exploration by educators and policy-makers of what constitutes excellence in bilingual education. Part of this ongoing exploration might include a focus on inspirational pedagogy and the creation of dual-language identity texts in order to showcase what a truly vibrant education for the 21st century might accomplish.

References

Cummins, J. (2007). Rethinking Monolingual Instructional Strategies in Multilingual Classrooms. *The Canadian Journal of Applied Linguistics*, 10 (2), 221–40.

Cummins, J. and Early, M. (2011). *Identity Texts: The Collaborative Creation of Power in Multilingual Schools*. Stoke-on-Trent: Trentham Books.

Lambert, W. E. (1984). An Overview of Issues in Immersion Education. In California State Department of Education (ed.), *Studies on Immersion Education: A Collection for United States Educators* (8–30). Sacramento: California State Department of Education.

Lambert, W. E. and Tucker, G. R. (1972). *Bilingual Education of Children. The St. Lambert experiment*. Rowley, Mass.: Newbury House.

JIM CUMMINS
University of Toronto

Further reading

Assessment

Black, P., Harrison, C., Lee, C., Marshall, B. and Wiliam, D. (2004). Working inside the Black Box: Assessment for Learning in the Classroom. *Phi Delta Kappan*, 86 (1), 8–21.

Martyniuk, W. (2010). *Aligning Tests with the CEFR: Reflections on Using the Council of Europe's Draft Manual*. Cambridge: Cambridge ESOL & Cambridge University Press.

Stobart, G. (2008). *Testing Time: The Uses and Abuses of Assessment*. London: Routledge.

Benefits of bilingualism

Beardsmore, H. B. (2008). Multilingualism, Cognition and Creativity. *International CLIL Research Journal* 1 (1), 4–19.

Bialystok, E., Craik, F. I. M. and Freedman, M. (2007). Bilingualism as a Protection against the Onset of Symptoms of Dementia. *Neuropsychologia*, 45, 459–64.

Mehisto, P. and Marsh, D. (2010). Approaching the Financial, Cognitive and Health Benefits of Bilingualism: Fuel for CLIL. In Y. Ruiz de Zarobe, J. Manuel Sierra and F. Gallardo del Puerto (eds.) *Content and Foreign Language Integrated Learning: Contributions to Multilingualism in European Contexts*. Frankfurt am Main: Peter Lang.

Bilingualism and bilingual education

Baker, C. (2011). *Foundations of Bilingual Education and Bilingualism (5th edn.)*. Bristol: Multilingual Matters.

Cummins, J. (2009). Bilingual and Immersion Programs. In M. H. Long, C. J. Doughty (eds.) *The Handbook of Language Teaching*. Malden, Mass.: Wiley-Blackwell, 161–81.

Cummins J. (2000). *Language, Power, and Pedagogy: Bilingual Children in the Crossfire*. Clevedon: Multilingual Matters.

García, O. (2009). *Bilingual Education in the 21st Century: A Global Perspective*. Oxford: Wiley-Blackwell.

Hornberger, N. H. (ed.) (2008). *Encyclopedia of Language and Education*. New York: Springer.

Lin, A.M.Y. and Man, E.Y.F. (2009). *Bilingual Education: Southeast Asian Perspectives*. Hong Kong: Hong Kong University Press.

Paradis, J., Genesee, F. and Crago, M. (2010). Dual Language Development and Disorders: A Handbook on Bilingualism and Second Language Learning (2nd edn.). Baltimore: Brookes Publishing. (Chapters 8 and 10 may be of particular interest.)

Tokuhama-Espinosa, T. (2008). *Living Languages: Multilingualism across the Lifespan*. Westport, Conn.: Praeger Publishers.

CLIL

Coyle D., Hood P. and Marsh D. (2010). *CLIL: Content and Language Integrated Learning*. Cambridge: Cambridge University Press.

Lyster, R. (2007). *Learning and Teaching Languages through Content: A Counterbalanced Approach*. Amsterdam: John Benjamins.

Mehisto, P., Marsh, D. and Frigols, M.-J. (2008). *Uncovering CLIL: Content and Language Integrated Learning in Bilingual and Multilingual Education*. Oxford: Macmillan.

English language learners

Cloud, N., Genesee, F. and Hamayan, E. (2009). *Literacy Instruction for English Language Learners*. Portsmouth, NH: Heinemann.

Francis, D. J., Lesaux, N. K. and August, D. L. (2006). Language of Instruction for Language Minority Learners. In D. L. August and T. Shanahan (eds.), *Developing Literacy in a Second Language: Report of the National Literacy Panel*. Mahwah, NJ: Lawrence Erlbaum Associates, 365–414.

Genesee, F. and Lindholm-Leary, K. J. (2011). The Education of English Language Learners. In K. Harris, S. Graham and T. Urdan (eds.), *APA Handbook of Educational Psychology*, vol. 3. Washington, DC: APA Books.

Gibbons, P. (2009). *English Learners, Academic Literacy, and Thinking: Learning in the Challenge Zone*. Portsmouth, NH: Heinemann.

Goldenberg, C. (2008). Teaching English Language Learners: What the Research Does – and Does Not – Say. *American Educator*, 32 (2) 8–23, 42–4.

Gender

Oates, T. 'Underachieving Boys' and 'Overachieving Girls' Revisited – Rhetoric and Reality (2007). In K. Myers, H. Taylors, S. Alder, and D. Leonard (eds) *Genderwatch: Still Watching... .* Stoke on Trent: Trentham Books.

Language diversity

Cummins, J. and Early, M. (2011). *Identity Texts: The Collaborative Creation of Power in Multilingual Schools*. Stoke on Trent: Trentham Books.

Edwards, J. (2010). *Language Diversity in the Classroom*. Bristol: Multilingual Matters.

Management, leadership and educational reform

Bishop, R., O'Sullivan, D. and Berryman, M. (2010). *Scaling Up Education Reform: Addressing the Politics of Disparity*. Wellington: New Zealand Council for Educational Research.

Leithwood, K., Harris, A. and Hopkins, D. (2008). Seven Strong Claims about Successful School Leadership. *School Leadership and Management* 28 (1) 27–42.

Spillane, J. P. and Diamond, J. B. (eds.). *Distributed Leadership in Practice*. New York: Teachers College Press.

Stoll, L., Bolam, R., McMahon, A. J., Thomas, S. M., Wallace, M., Greenwood, A. and Hackey, K.M. (2006). *Professional Learning Communities: Source Materials for School Leaders and Other Leaders of Professional Learning. Booklet 1: User Guide: Getting Started and Thinking about Your Journey*. London: DfES Innovation Unit, National College for School Leadership and General Teaching Council.

Meta-studies in education

Hattie, J. (2009). *Visible Learning: A Synthesis of over 800 Meta-analyses Relating to Achievement*. Oxford: Routledge.

Index